Connected  Mathematics 2™

Frogs, Fleas, and Painted Cubes

Quadratic Relationships

$y = x^2 + x - 6$

Glenda Lappan

James T. Fey

William M. Fitzgerald

Susan N. Friel

Elizabeth Difanis Phillips

PEARSON

Boston, Massachusetts · Glenview, Illinois · Shoreview, Minnesota · Upper Saddle River, New Jersey

Connected Mathematics™ was developed at Michigan State University with financial support from the Michigan State University Office of the Provost, Computing and Technology, and the College of Natural Science.

This material is based upon work supported by the National Science Foundation under Grant No. MDR 9150217 and Grant No. ESI 9986372. Opinions expressed are those of the authors and not necessarily those of the Foundation.

The Michigan State University authors and administration have agreed that all MSU royalties arising from this publication will be devoted to purposes supported by the MSU Mathematics Education Enrichment Fund.

13-digit ISBN 978-0-13-366152-1
10-digit ISBN 0-13-366152-0
1 2 3 4 5 6 7 8 9 10   11 10 09 08

Authors of Connected Mathematics

(from left to right) Glenda Lappan, Betty Phillips, Susan Friel, Bill Fitzgerald, Jim Fey

Glenda Lappan is a University Distinguished Professor in the Department of Mathematics at Michigan State University. Her research and development interests are in the connected areas of students' learning of mathematics and mathematics teachers' professional growth and change related to the development and enactment of K–12 curriculum materials.

James T. Fey is a Professor of Curriculum and Instruction and Mathematics at the University of Maryland. His consistent professional interest has been development and research focused on curriculum materials that engage middle and high school students in problem-based collaborative investigations of mathematical ideas and their applications.

William M. Fitzgerald *(Deceased)* was a Professor in the Department of Mathematics at Michigan State University. His early research was on the use of concrete materials in supporting student learning and led to the development of teaching materials for laboratory environments. Later he helped develop a teaching model to support student experimentation with mathematics.

Susan N. Friel is a Professor of Mathematics Education in the School of Education at the University of North Carolina at Chapel Hill. Her research interests focus on statistics education for middle-grade students and, more broadly, on teachers' professional development and growth in teaching mathematics K–8.

Elizabeth Difanis Phillips is a Senior Academic Specialist in the Mathematics Department of Michigan State University. She is interested in teaching and learning mathematics for both teachers and students. These interests have led to curriculum and professional development projects at the middle school and high school levels, as well as projects related to the teaching and learning of algebra across the grades.

Field Test Sites for CMP2

During the development of the revised edition of *Connected Mathematics* (CMP2), more than 100 classroom teachers have field-tested materials at 49 school sites in 12 states and the District of Columbia. This classroom testing occurred over three academic years (2001 through 2004), allowing careful study of the effectiveness of each of the 24 units that comprise the program. A special thanks to the students and teachers at these pilot schools.

Arkansas
Magnolia Public Schools
Kittena Bell*, Judith Trowell*; *Central Elementary School:* Maxine Broom, Betty Eddy, Tiffany Fallin, Bonnie Flurry, Carolyn Monk, Elizabeth Tye; *Magnolia Junior High School:* Monique Bryan, Ginger Cook, David Graham, Shelby Lamkin

Colorado
Boulder Public Schools
Nevin Platt Middle School: Judith Koenig

St. Vrain Valley School District, Longmont
Westview Middle School: Colleen Beyer, Kitty Canupp, Ellie Decker*, Peggy McCarthy, Tanya deNobrega, Cindy Payne, Ericka Pilon, Andrew Roberts

District of Columbia
Capitol Hill Day School: Ann Lawrence

Georgia
University of Georgia, Athens
Brad Findell

Madison Public Schools
Morgan County Middle School: Renee Burgdorf, Lynn Harris, Nancy Kurtz, Carolyn Stewart

Maine
Falmouth Public Schools
Falmouth Middle School: Donna Erikson, Joyce Hebert, Paula Hodgkins, Rick Hogan, David Legere, Cynthia Martin, Barbara Stiles, Shawn Towle*

---

* indicates a Field Test Site Coordinator

Michigan
Portland Public Schools
Portland Middle School: Mark Braun, Holly DeRosia, Kathy Dole*, Angie Foote, Teri Keusch, Tammi Wardwell

Traverse City Area Public Schools
Bertha Vos Elementary: Kristin Sak; *Central Grade School:* Michelle Clark; Jody Meyers; *Eastern Elementary:* Karrie Tufts; *Interlochen Elementary:* Mary McGee-Cullen; *Long Lake Elementary:* Julie Faulkner*, Charlie Maxbauer, Katherine Sleder; *Norris Elementary:* Hope Slanaker; *Oak Park Elementary:* Jessica Steed; *Traverse Heights Elementary:* Jennifer Wolfert; *Westwoods Elementary:* Nancy Conn; *Old Mission Peninsula School:* Deb Larimer; *Traverse City East Junior High:* Ivanka Berkshire, Ruthanne Kladder, Jan Palkowski, Jane Peterson, Mary Beth Schmitt; *Traverse City West Junior High:* Dan Fouch*, Ray Fouch

Sturgis Public Schools
Sturgis Middle School: Ellen Eisele

Minnesota
Burnsville School District 191
Hidden Valley Elementary: Stephanie Cin, Jane McDevitt

Hopkins School District 270
Alice Smith Elementary: Sandra Cowing, Kathleen Gustafson, Martha Mason, Scott Stillman; *Eisenhower Elementary:* Chad Bellig, Patrick Berger, Nancy Glades, Kye Johnson, Shane Wasserman, Victoria Wilson; *Gatewood Elementary:* Sarah Ham, Julie Kloos, Janine Pung, Larry Wade; *Glen Lake Elementary:* Jacqueline Cramer, Kathy Hering, Cecelia Morris,

Robb Trenda; *Katherine Curren Elementary:* Diane Bancroft, Sue DeWit, John Wilson; *L. H. Tanglen Elementary:* Kevin Athmann, Lisa Becker, Mary LaBelle, Kathy Rezac, Roberta Severson; *Meadowbrook Elementary:* Jan Gauger, Hildy Shank, Jessica Zimmerman; *North Junior High:* Laurel Hahn, Kristin Lee, Jodi Markuson, Bruce Mestemacher, Laurel Miller, Bonnie Rinker, Jeannine Salzer, Sarah Shafer, Cam Stottler; *West Junior High:* Alicia Beebe, Kristie Earl, Nobu Fujii, Pam Georgetti, Susan Gilbert, Regina Nelson Johnson, Debra Lindstrom, Michele Luke*, Jon Sorenson

Minneapolis School District 1
Ann Sullivan K-8 School: Bronwyn Collins; Anne Bartel* (Curriculum and Instruction Office)

Wayzata School District 284
Central Middle School: Sarajane Myers, Dan Nielsen, Tanya Ravenholdt

White Bear Lake School District 624
Central Middle School: Amy Jorgenson, Michelle Reich, Brenda Sammon

New York
New York City Public Schools
IS 89: Yelena Aynbinder, Chi-Man Ng, Nina Rapaport, Joel Spengler, Phyllis Tam*, Brent Wyso; *Wagner Middle School:* Jason Appel, Intissar Fernandez, Yee Gee Get, Richard Goldstein, Irving Marcus, Sue Norton, Bernadita Owens, Jennifer Rehn*, Kevin Yuhas

Ohio

Talawanda School District, Oxford
Talawanda Middle School: Teresa Abrams, Larry Brock, Heather Brosey, Julie Churchman, Monna Even, Karen Fitch, Bob George, Amanda Klee, Pat Meade, Sandy Montgomery, Barbara Sherman, Lauren Steidl

Miami University
Jeffrey Wanko*

Springfield Public Schools
Rockway School: Jim Mamer

Pennsylvania

Pittsburgh Public Schools
Kenneth Labuskes, Marianne O'Connor, Mary Lynn Raith*; *Arthur J. Rooney Middle School:* David Hairston, Stamatina Mousetis, Alfredo Zangaro; *Frick International Studies Academy:* Suzanne Berry, Janet Falkowski, Constance Finseth, Romika Hodge, Frank Machi; *Reizenstein Middle School:* Jeff Baldwin, James Brautigam, Lorena Burnett, Glen Cobbett, Michael Jordan, Margaret Lazur, Melissa Munnell, Holly Neely, Ingrid Reed, Dennis Reft

Texas

Austin Independent School District
Bedichek Middle School: Lisa Brown, Jennifer Glasscock, Vicki Massey

El Paso Independent School District
Cordova Middle School: Armando Aguirre, Anneliesa Durkes, Sylvia Guzman, Pat Holguin*, William Holguin, Nancy Nava, Laura Orozco, Michelle Peña, Roberta Rosen, Patsy Smith, Jeremy Wolf

Plano Independent School District
Patt Henry, James Wohlgehagen*; *Frankford Middle School:* Mandy Baker, Cheryl Butsch, Amy Dudley, Betsy Eshelman, Janet Greene, Cort Haynes, Kathy Letchworth, Kay Marshall, Kelly McCants, Amy Reck, Judy Scott, Syndy Snyder, Lisa Wang; *Wilson Middle School:* Darcie Bane, Amanda Bedenko, Whitney Evans, Tonelli Hatley, Sarah (Becky) Higgs, Kelly Johnston, Rebecca McElligott, Kay Neuse, Cheri Slocum, Kelli Straight

Washington

Evergreen School District
Shahala Middle School: Nicole Abrahamsen, Terry Coon*, Carey Doyle, Sheryl Drechsler, George Gemma, Gina Helland, Amy Hilario, Darla Lidyard, Sean McCarthy, Tilly Meyer, Willow Neuwelt, Todd Parsons, Brian Pederson, Stan Posey, Shawn Scott, Craig Sjoberg, Lynette Sundstrom, Charles Switzer, Luke Youngblood

Wisconsin

Beaver Dam Unified School District
Beaver Dam Middle School: Jim Braemer, Jeanne Frick, Jessica Greatens, Barbara Link, Dennis McCormick, Karen Michels, Nancy Nichols*, Nancy Palm, Shelly Stelsel, Susan Wiggins

---

* indicates a Field Test Site Coordinator

Reviews of CMP to Guide Development of CMP2

Before writing for CMP2 began or field tests were conducted, the first edition of *Connected Mathematics* was submitted to the mathematics faculties of school districts from many parts of the country and to 80 individual reviewers for extensive comments.

School District Survey Reviews of CMP

Arizona
Madison School District #38 (Phoenix)

Arkansas
Cabot School District, Little Rock School District, Magnolia School District

California
Los Angeles Unified School District

Colorado
St. Vrain Valley School District (Longmont)

Florida
Leon County Schools (Tallahassee)

Illinois
School District #21 (Wheeling)

Indiana
Joseph L. Block Junior High (East Chicago)

Kentucky
Fayette County Public Schools (Lexington)

Maine
Selection of Schools

Massachusetts
Selection of Schools

Michigan
Sparta Area Schools

Minnesota
Hopkins School District

Texas
Austin Independent School District, The El Paso Collaborative for Academic Excellence, Plano Independent School District

Wisconsin
Platteville Middle School

Individual Reviewers of CMP

Arkansas
Deborah Cramer; Robby Frizzell *(Taylor)*; Lowell Lynde *(University of Arkansas, Monticello)*; Leigh Manzer *(Norfork)*; Lynne Roberts *(Emerson High School, Emerson)*; Tony Timms *(Cabot Public Schools)*; Judith Trowell *(Arkansas Department of Higher Education)*

California
José Alcantar *(Gilroy)*; Eugenie Belcher *(Gilroy)*; Marian Pasternack *(Lowman M. S. T. Center, North Hollywood)*; Susana Pezoa *(San Jose)*; Todd Rabusin *(Hollister)*; Margaret Siegfried *(Ocala Middle School, San Jose)*; Polly Underwood *(Ocala Middle School, San Jose)*

Colorado
Janeane Golliher *(St. Vrain Valley School District, Longmont)*; Judith Koenig *(Nevin Platt Middle School, Boulder)*

Florida
Paige Loggins *(Swift Creek Middle School, Tallahassee)*

Illinois
Jan Robinson *(School District #21, Wheeling)*

Indiana
Frances Jackson *(Joseph L. Block Junior High, East Chicago)*

Kentucky
Natalee Feese *(Fayette County Public Schools, Lexington)*

Maine
Betsy Berry *(Maine Math & Science Alliance, Augusta)*

Maryland
Joseph Gagnon *(University of Maryland, College Park)*; Paula Maccini *(University of Maryland, College Park)*

Massachusetts
George Cobb *(Mt. Holyoke College, South Hadley)*; Cliff Kanold *(University of Massachusetts, Amherst)*

Michigan
Mary Bouck *(Farwell Area Schools)*; Carol Dorer *(Slauson Middle School, Ann Arbor)*; Carrie Heaney *(Forsythe Middle School, Ann Arbor)*; Ellen Hopkins *(Clague Middle School, Ann Arbor)*; Teri Keusch *(Portland Middle School, Portland)*; Valerie Mills *(Oakland Schools, Waterford)*; Mary Beth Schmitt *(Traverse City East Junior High, Traverse City)*; Jack Smith *(Michigan State University, East Lansing)*; Rebecca Spencer *(Sparta Middle School, Sparta)*; Ann Marie Nicoll Turner *(Tappan Middle School, Ann Arbor)*; Scott Turner *(Scarlett Middle School, Ann Arbor)*

Minnesota
Margarita Alvarez *(Olson Middle School, Minneapolis)*; Jane Amundson *(Nicollet Junior High, Burnsville)*; Anne Bartel *(Minneapolis Public Schools)*; Gwen Ranzau Campbell *(Sunrise Park Middle School, White Bear Lake)*; Stephanie Cin *(Hidden Valley Elementary, Burnsville)*; Joan Garfield *(University of Minnesota, Minneapolis)*; Gretchen Hall *(Richfield Middle School, Richfield)*; Jennifer Larson *(Olson Middle School, Minneapolis)*; Michele Luke *(West Junior High, Minnetonka)*; Jeni Meyer *(Richfield Junior High, Richfield)*; Judy Pfingsten *(Inver Grove Heights Middle School, Inver Grove Heights)*; Sarah Shafer *(North Junior High, Minnetonka)*; Genni Steele *(Central Middle School, White Bear Lake)*; Victoria Wilson *(Eisenhower Elementary, Hopkins)*; Paul Zorn *(St. Olaf College, Northfield)*

New York
Debra Altenau-Bartolino *(Greenwich Village Middle School, New York)*; Doug Clements *(University of Buffalo)*; Francis Curcio *(New York University, New York)*; Christine Dorosh *(Clinton School for Writers, Brooklyn)*; Jennifer Rehn *(East Side Middle School, New York)*; Phyllis Tam *(IS 89 Lab School, New York)*;

Marie Turini *(Louis Armstrong Middle School, New York)*; Lucy West *(Community School District 2, New York)*; Monica Witt *(Simon Baruch Intermediate School 104, New York)*

Pennsylvania
Robert Aglietti *(Pittsburgh)*; Sharon Mihalich *(Pittsburgh)*; Jennifer Plumb *(South Hills Middle School, Pittsburgh)*; Mary Lynn Raith *(Pittsburgh Public Schools)*

Texas
Michelle Bittick *(Austin Independent School District)*; Margaret Cregg *(Plano Independent School District)*; Sheila Cunningham *(Klein Independent School District)*; Judy Hill *(Austin Independent School District)*; Patricia Holguin *(El Paso Independent School District)*; Bonnie McNemar *(Arlington)*; Kay Neuse *(Plano Independent School District)*; Joyce Polanco *(Austin Independent School District)*; Marge Ramirez *(University of Texas at El Paso)*; Pat Rossman *(Baker Campus, Austin)*; Cindy Schimek *(Houston)*; Cynthia Schneider *(Charles A. Dana Center, University of Texas at Austin)*; Uri Treisman *(Charles A. Dana Center, University of Texas at Austin)*; Jacqueline Weilmuenster *(Grapevine-Colleyville Independent School District)*; LuAnn Weynand *(San Antonio)*; Carmen Whitman *(Austin Independent School District)*; James Wohlgehagen *(Plano Independent School District)*

Washington
Ramesh Gangolli *(University of Washington, Seattle)*

Wisconsin
Susan Lamon *(Marquette University, Hales Corner)*; Steve Reinhart *(retired, Chippewa Falls Middle School, Eau Claire)*

Table of Contents

Frogs, Fleas, and Painted Cubes
Quadratic Relationships

Frogs, Fleas, and Painted Cubes

Quadratic Relationships

Suppose you travel to Mars to prospect a precious metal. You can claim any rectangular piece of land you can surround by 20 meters of laser fencing. How should you arrange your fencing to enclose the maximum area?

After a victory, team members exchange high fives. How many high fives are exchanged among a team with 5 players? With 6 players? With *n* players?

A ball is thrown into the air. Its height *h* in feet after *t* seconds is modeled by the equation $h = -16t^2 + 64t$. What is the maximum height the ball reaches? When does it reach this height?

Mathematics is useful for solving practical problems in science, business, engineering, and economics. In earlier units, you studied problems that could be modeled with linear or exponential relationships. In this unit, you will explore quadratic relationships. Quadratic relationships are found in many interesting situations, such as the path of flares and rockets launched from the ground as well as the situations on the previous page.

Mathematical Highlights

Quadratic Relationships

In *Frogs, Fleas, and Painted Cubes,* you will explore quadratic functions, an important type of nonlinear relationship.

You will learn how to

- Recognize patterns of change for quadratic relationships
- Write equations for quadratic relationships represented in tables, graphs, and problem situations
- Connect quadratic equations to the patterns in tables and graphs of quadratic relationships
- Use a quadratic equation to identify the maximum or minimum value, the *x*- and *y*-intercepts, and other important features of the graph of the equation
- Recognize equivalent quadratic expressions
- Use the Distributive Property to write equivalent quadratic expressions in factored and expanded form
- Use tables, graphs, and equations of quadratic relationships to solve problems in a variety of situations from geometry, science, and business
- Compare properties of quadratic, linear, and exponential relationships

As you work on problems in this unit, ask yourself questions about problem situations that involve nonlinear relationships:

What are the variables?

How can I recognize whether the relationship between the variables is quadratic?

What equation models a quadratic relationship in a table, graph, or problem context?

How can I answer questions about the situation by studying a table, graph, or equation of the quadratic relationship?

Investigation 1

Introduction to Quadratic Relationships

In January of 1848, gold was discovered near Sacramento, California. By the spring of that year, a great gold rush had begun, bringing 250,000 new residents to California.

Throughout history, people have moved to particular areas of the world with hopes of improving their lives.

- In 1867, prospectors headed to South Africa in search of diamonds.
- From 1860 to 1900, farmers headed to the American prairie where land was free.
- The 1901 Spindletop oil gusher brought drillers by the thousands to eastern Texas.

Prospectors and farmers had to stake claims on the land they wanted to work.

1.1 Staking a Claim

Suppose it is the year 2100, and a rare and precious metal has just been discovered on Mars. You and hundreds of other adventurers travel to the planet to stake your claim. You are allowed to claim any rectangular piece of land that can be surrounded by 20 meters of laser fencing. You want to arrange your fencing to enclose the maximum area possible.

Problem 1.1 Maximizing Area

A. Sketch several rectangles with a fixed perimeter of 20 meters. Include some with small areas and some with large areas. Label the dimensions of each rectangle.

B. Make a table showing the length, width, and area for every rectangle with a perimeter of 20 meters and whole-number side lengths. Describe some patterns that you observe in the table.

C. Make a graph of the (*length, area*) data. Describe the shape of the graph.

D. 1. What rectangle dimensions give the greatest possible area? Explain.

2. Suppose the dimensions were not restricted to whole numbers. Would this change your answer? Explain.

ACE Homework starts on page 11.

For: Stat Tools
Visit: PHSchool.com
Web Code: apd-4101

1.2 Reading Graphs and Tables

The relationship between length and area in Problem 1.1 is a **quadratic relationship.** Quadratic relationships are characterized by their U-shaped graphs, which are called **parabolas.**

In Problem 1.1, the area depends on, or is a *function* of, the length. Recall that a relationship in which one variable depends on another is a **function.** In this case, the relationship is a quadratic function. A more precise definition of functions will be discussed in later mathematics courses.

Many of the relationships you studied in earlier units are functions. For example,

- The distance covered by a van traveling at a constant speed is a function of time. The relationship between time and distance is a linear function.

- The value of an investment that grows at 4% per year is a function of the number of years. The relationship between the number of years and the value is an exponential function.

You have learned about the characteristics of the tables, graphs, and equations of linear and exponential functions. As you explore quadratic functions in this unit, look for common patterns in the tables, graphs, and equations.

Problem 1.2 Reading Graphs and Tables

The graph and table show length and area data for rectangles with a certain fixed perimeter.

A. **1.** Describe the shape of the graph and any special features you see.

2. What is the greatest area possible for a rectangle with this perimeter? What are the dimensions of this rectangle?

3. What is the area of the rectangle whose length is 10 meters? What is the area of the rectangle whose length is 30 meters? How are these rectangles related?

4. What are the dimensions of the rectangle with an area of 175 square meters?

5. What is the fixed perimeter for the rectangles represented by the graph? Explain how you found the perimeter.

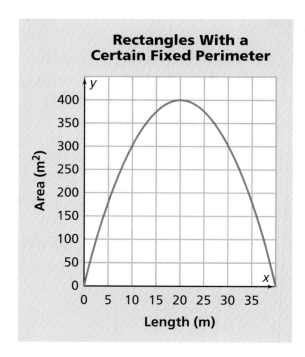

Rectangles With a Certain Fixed Perimeter

B. Use the table to answer parts (1)–(5).

1. What patterns do you observe in the table? Compare these patterns with those you observed in the graph in Question A.

2. What is the fixed perimeter for the rectangles represented by this table? Explain.

3. What is the greatest area possible for a rectangle with this perimeter? What are the dimensions of this rectangle?

4. Estimate the dimensions of a rectangle with this fixed perimeter and an area of 16 square meters.

5. Suppose a rectangle with this perimeter has an area of 35.5 square meters. What are its dimensions?

Rectangles With a Certain Fixed Perimeter

Length (m)	Area (m²)
0	0
1	11
2	20
3	27
4	32
5	35
6	36
7	35
8	32
9	27
10	20
11	11
12	0

ACE Homework starts on page 11.

1.3 Writing an Equation

You used tables and graphs to represent relationships between length and area for rectangles with fixed perimeters. In this problem, you will write equations for these relationships.

Getting Ready for Problem 1.3

You know that the formula for the area A of a rectangle with length ℓ and width w is $A = \ell w$ and the formula for perimeter P is $P = 2\ell + 2w$.

The rectangle below has a perimeter of 20 meters and a length of ℓ meters.

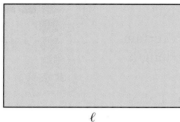

ℓ

- Use the fixed perimeter to express the width of this rectangle in terms of ℓ.
- Write an equation for the area using A and ℓ as the only variables.

Problem 1.3 Writing an Equation

A. Consider rectangles with a perimeter of 60 meters.

1. Sketch a rectangle to represent this situation. Label one side ℓ. Express the width in terms of ℓ.

2. Write an equation for the area A in terms of ℓ.

3. Use a calculator to make a table for your equation. Use your table to estimate the maximum area. What dimensions correspond to this area?

4. Use a calculator or data from your table to help you sketch a graph of the relationship between length and area.

5. How can you use your graph to find the maximum area possible? How does your graph show the length that corresponds to the maximum area?

B. The equation for the areas of rectangles with a certain fixed perimeter is $A = \ell(35 - \ell)$, where ℓ is the length in meters.

1. Draw a rectangle to represent this situation. Label one side ℓ. Label the other sides in terms of ℓ.

2. Make a table showing the length, width, and area for lengths of 0, 5, 10, 15, 20, 25, 30, and 35 meters. What patterns do you see?

3. Describe the graph of this equation.

4. What is the maximum area? What dimensions correspond to this maximum area? Explain.

5. Describe two ways you could find the fixed perimeter. What is the perimeter?

C. Suppose you know the perimeter of a rectangle. How can you write an equation for the area in terms of the length of a side?

D. Study the graphs, tables, and equations for areas of rectangles with fixed perimeters. Which representation is most useful for finding the maximum area? Which is most useful for finding the fixed perimeter?

active math
online

For: Algebra Tools
Visit: PHSchool.com
Web Code: apd-4103

ACE Homework starts on page 11.

Applications

1. Find the maximum area for a rectangle with a perimeter of 120 meters. Make your answer convincing by including these things:

- Sketches of rectangles with a perimeter of 120 meters (Include rectangles that do not have the maximum area and the rectangle you think does have the maximum area.)

- A table of lengths and areas for rectangles with a perimeter of 120 meters (Use increments of 5 meters for the lengths.)

- A graph of the relationship between length and area

Explain how each piece of evidence supports your answer.

2. What is the maximum area for a rectangle with a perimeter of 130 meters? As in Exercise 1, support your answer with sketches, a table, and a graph.

3. The graph shows the length and area of rectangles with a fixed perimeter. Use the graph for parts (a)–(e).

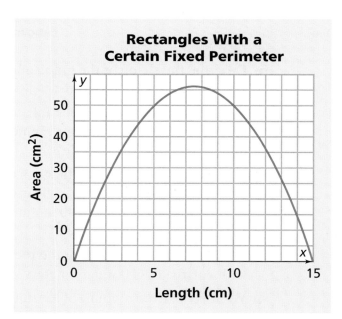

Rectangles With a Certain Fixed Perimeter

a. Describe the shape of the graph and any special features.

b. What is the maximum area for a rectangle with this fixed perimeter? What are the dimensions of this rectangle?

c. Is there a rectangle with the least possible area? Explain.

d. What is the area of a rectangle with a length of 3 centimeters?

e. Describe two ways to find the fixed perimeter for the rectangles represented by the graph.

4. A farm wants to add a small, rectangular petting zoo for the public. They have a fixed amount of fencing to use for the zoo. This graph shows the lengths and areas of the rectangles they can make.

Rectangular Petting Zoos

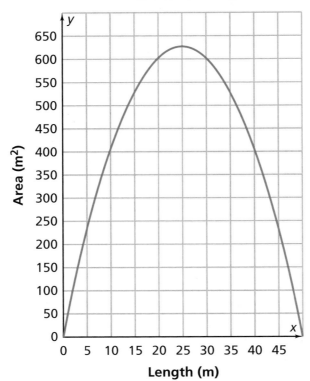

a. Describe the shape of the graph and any special features you observe.

b. What is the greatest area possible for a rectangle with this perimeter? What are the dimensions of this rectangle?

c. What is the area of the rectangle with a length of 10 meters? What is the area of the rectangle with a length of 40 meters? How are these rectangles related?

d. What are the dimensions of the rectangle with an area of 600 square meters?

e. What is the fixed amount of fencing available for the petting zoo? Explain.

5. The lifeguards at a beach want to place a rectangular boundary around the swimming area that can be used for water basketball. They have a fixed amount of rope to make the boundary. They use the table at the right to look at possible arrangements.

Length (m)	Area (m²)
1	15
2	28
3	39
4	48
5	55
6	60
7	63
8	64
9	63
10	60
11	55
12	48
13	39
14	28
15	15

a. What patterns do you observe in the table?

b. What is the fixed perimeter for the possible swimming areas?

c. Sketch a graph of the (*length, area*) data. Describe the shape of the graph.

d. Suppose the lifeguards make a rectangle with an area of 11.5 square meters. What are the dimensions of the rectangle?

e. The lifeguards want to enclose the greatest area possible. What should be the dimensions of the swimming area?

6. a. A rectangle has a perimeter of 30 meters and a side length of ℓ. Express the lengths of the other sides of the rectangle in terms of ℓ.

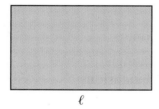

ℓ

b. Write an equation for the area A in terms of ℓ.

c. Make a graph of your equation and describe its shape.

d. Use your equation to find the area of the rectangle with a length of 10 meters.

e. How could you find the area in part (d) by using your graph?

f. How could you find the area in part (d) by using a table?

g. What is the maximum area possible for a rectangle with a perimeter of 30 meters? What are the dimensions of this rectangle?

7. a. A rectangle has a perimeter of 50 meters and a side length of ℓ. Express the lengths of the other sides of the rectangle in terms of ℓ.

   b. Write an equation for the area A in terms of ℓ.

   c. Sketch a graph of your equation and describe its shape.

   d. Use your equation to find the area of the rectangle with a length of 10 meters.

   e. How could you find the area in part (d) by using your graph?

   f. How could you find the area in part (d) by using a table?

   g. What is the maximum area possible for a rectangle with a perimeter of 50 meters? What are the dimensions of this rectangle?

8. The equation for the areas of rectangles with a certain fixed perimeter is $A = \ell(20 - \ell)$, where ℓ is the length in meters.

For: Help with Exercise 8
Web Code: ape-4108

   a. Describe the graph of this equation.

   b. What is the maximum area for a rectangle with this perimeter? What dimensions correspond to this area? Explain.

   c. A rectangle with this perimeter has a length of 15 meters. What is its area?

   d. Describe two ways you can find the perimeter. What is the perimeter?

9. a. Copy and complete the graph to show areas for rectangles with a certain fixed perimeter and lengths greater than 3 meters.

   b. Make a table of data for this situation.

   c. What is the maximum area for a rectangle with this perimeter? What are the dimensions of this rectangle?

10. Multiple Choice Which equation describes the graph in Exercise 9?

   A. $A = \ell(\ell - 6)$ **B.** $A = \ell(12 - \ell)$

   C. $A = \ell(6 - \ell)$ **D.** $A = \ell(3 - \ell)$

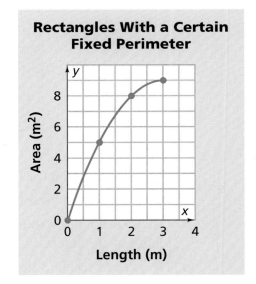

Rectangles With a Certain Fixed Perimeter

11. a. Copy and complete the table to show areas for rectangles with a certain fixed perimeter and lengths greater than 4 m.

b. Make a graph of the relationship between length and area.

c. What are the dimensions of the rectangle with the maximum area?

12. Multiple Choice Which equation describes the table in Exercise 11?

F. $A = \ell(8 - \ell)$ **G.** $A = \ell(16 - \ell)$

H. $A = \ell(4 - \ell)$ **J.** $A = \ell(\ell - 8)$

Rectangles With a Certain Fixed Perimeter

Length (m)	Area (m²)
0	0
1	7
2	12
3	15
4	16
5	▩
6	▩
7	▩
8	▩

13. The equation $p = d(100 - d)$ gives the monthly profit p a photographer will earn if she charges d dollars for each print.

a. Make a table and a graph for this equation.

b. Estimate the price that will produce the maximum profit. Explain.

c. How are the table and graph for this situation similar to those you made in Problem 1.1? How are they different?

Connections

14. Of all the rectangles with whole-number side lengths and an area of 20 square centimeters, which has the least perimeter? Explain.

15. Multiple Choice What does $2(-3 + 5) + 7 \times -4 + -1$ equal?

 A. -45 **B.** -31 **C.** -55 **D.** -25

16. Eduardo's neighborhood association subdivided a large rectangular field into two playing fields as shown in the diagram.

 a. Write expressions showing two ways you could calculate the area of the large field.

 b. Use the diagram and your expressions in part (a) to explain the Distributive Property.

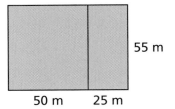

55 m

50 m 25 m

For Exercises 17–20, use the Distributive Property to write the expression in expanded form. Then, simplify.

17. $21(5 + 6)$ **18.** $2(35 + 1)$ **19.** $12(10 - 2)$ **20.** $9(3 + 5)$

For Exercises 21–23, use the Distributive Property to write the expression in factored form.

21. $15 + 6$ **22.** $42 + 27$ **23.** $12 + 120$

Go Online
PHSchool.com

For: Multiple-Choice Skills
Practice
Web Code: apa-4154

For Exercises 24 and 25, solve each equation for x.

24. $5x - 30 = 95$ **25.** $22 + 4x = 152 - 9x$

For Exercises 26 and 27,

 • **Describe the pattern of change for the relationship.**

 • **Describe how the pattern of change would look in a graph and in a table. Give as many details as you can without making a graph or table.**

26. $y = 5x + 12$ **27.** $y = 10 - 3x$

28. A rectangular field has a perimeter of 300 yards. The equation $l = 150 - w$ represents the relationship between the length l and width w of the field.

 a. Explain why the equation is correct.

 b. Is the relationship between length and width quadratic? Explain.

16 Frogs, Fleas, and Painted Cubes

c. Suppose a field is a nonrectangular parallelogram with a perimeter of 300 yards. Is the relationship between the lengths of adjacent sides the same as it is for the rectangular field?

d. Suppose a field is a quadrilateral that is not a parallelogram. The perimeter of the field is 300 yards. Is the relationship between the lengths of adjacent sides the same as it is for the rectangular field?

29. Mr. DeAngelo is designing a school building. The music room floor will be a rectangle with an area of 1,200 square feet.

a. Make a table with ten rows showing a range of possible lengths and widths for the music room floor.

b. Add a column to your table for the perimeter of each rectangle.

c. What patterns do you see in the perimeter column? What kinds of rectangles have large perimeters? What kinds have smaller perimeters?

d. Write an equation you can use to calculate the length of the floor for any given width.

Extensions

30. A beach has a rectangular swimming area for toddlers. One side of the swimming area is the shore. Buoys and a rope with a length of 20 meters are used to form the other three sides.

a. How should the rope be arranged to create a rectangle with the maximum area?

b. In Problem 1.1, a fixed perimeter of 20 meters is also used to form a rectangle. Compare the rectangle with maximum area in that problem to the rectangle with maximum area in part (a). Are the shapes and areas of the rectangles the same? Explain.

c. Make a graph relating the length and area for the possible rectangular swimming areas. How does the graph compare with the graph from Problem 1.1?

Mathematical Reflections 1

In this investigation, you looked at the relationship between length and area for rectangles with a fixed perimeter. You learned that this relationship is a quadratic function. The following questions will help you summarize what you have learned.

Think about your answers to these questions. Discuss your ideas with other students and your teacher. Then, write a summary of your findings in your notebook.

1. **a.** Describe the characteristics of graphs and tables of quadratic functions you have observed so far.

   b. How do the patterns in a graph of a quadratic function appear in the table of values for the function?

2. Describe two ways to find the maximum area for rectangles with a fixed perimeter.

3. How are tables, graphs, and equations for quadratic functions different from those for linear and exponential functions?

Quadratic Expressions

Suppose you give a friend two $1 bills, and your friend gives you eight quarters. You would consider this a fair trade. Sometimes it is not this easy to determine whether a trade is fair.

2.1 Trading Land

Getting Ready for Problem 2.1

- A developer has purchased all of the land on a mall site except for one square lot. The lot measures 125 meters on each side. In exchange for the lot, the developer offers its owner a lot on another site. The plan for this lot is shown below. Do you think this is a fair trade?

225 m

25 m

lot offered by the developer

125 m

125 m

lot on mall site

In this problem, you will look at a trade situation. See if you can find a pattern that will help you make predictions about more complex situations.

Problem 2.1 Representing Areas of Rectangles

Suppose you trade a square lot for a rectangular lot. The length of the rectangular lot is 2 meters greater than the side length of the square lot, and the width is 2 meters less.

A. 1. Copy and complete the table.

Original Square		New Rectangle			Difference in Areas (m^2)
Side Length (m)	Area (m^2)	Length (m)	Width (m)	Area (m^2)	
2	4	4	0	0	4
3	9	5	1	5	4
4	▨	▨	▨	▨	▨
5	▨	▨	▨	▨	▨
6	▨	▨	▨	▨	▨
n	▨	▨	▨	▨	▨

2. Explain why the table starts with a side length of 2 meters, rather than 0 meters or 1 meter.

3. For each side length, tell how the areas of the new and original lots compare. For which side lengths, if any, is the trade fair?

B. 1. Write an equation for the relationship between the side length n and the area A_1 of the original lot.

2. Write an equation for the relationship between the side length n of the original lot and the area A_2 of the new lot.

3. Carl claims there are two different expressions for the area of the new lot. Is this possible? Explain.

C. 1. On the same axes, sketch graphs of the area equations for both lots. For the independent variable, show values from -10 to 10. For the dependent variable, show values from -10 to 30.

2. For each graph, tell which part of the graph makes sense for the situation.

3. Describe any similarities and differences in the two graphs.

D. Are either of the relationships quadratic relationships? Explain.

ACE Homework starts on page 30.

2.2 Changing One Dimension

The expression $(n - 2)(n + 2)$ is in **factored form** because it is written as a product of factors. The expression $n^2 - 4$ is in **expanded form** because it is written as the sum or difference of terms. A **term** is an expression that consists of variables and/or numbers multiplied together. Specifically, $n^2 - 4$ is the difference of the terms n^2 and 4.

The expressions $(n - 2)(n + 2)$ and $n^2 - 4$ are *equivalent*. This means $(n - 2)(n + 2) = n^2 - 4$ is true for every value of n.

Getting Ready for Problem 2.2

A square has sides of lengths x centimeters. One dimension of the square is increased by 3 centimeters to make a new rectangle.

- How do the areas of the square and the new rectangle compare?

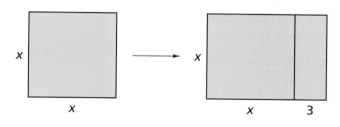

- Write two expressions for the area of the new rectangle. How do you know that the expressions are equivalent?

The expressions $x(x + 3)$ and $x^2 + 3x$ are examples of quadratic expressions. An expression in factored form is quadratic if it has exactly two linear factors, each with the variable raised to the first power. An expression in expanded form is quadratic if the highest power of the variable is 2.

A. Each diagram shows a large rectangle divided into two smaller rectangles. Write two expressions, one in factored form and one in expanded form, for the area of the rectangle outlined in red.

1.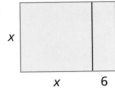

2.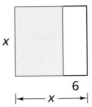

B. Complete the steps in bullets for each of the factored expressions in parts (1)–(3).

  ● Draw a divided rectangle whose area is represented by the expression. Label the lengths and area of each section.

  ● Write an equivalent expression in expanded form.

  1. $x(x + 4)$ **2.** $x(x - 4)$ **3.** $x(5 + 2)$

C. Complete the steps in bullets for each of the factored expressions in parts (1)–(3).

  ● Draw a divided rectangle whose area is represented by the expression. Label the lengths and area of each section.

  ● Tell what clues in the expanded expression helped you draw the divided rectangle.

  ● Write an equivalent expression in factored form.

  1. $x^2 + 5x$ **2.** $x^2 - 5x$ **3.** $5x + 4x$

ACE **Homework starts on page 30.**

2.3 Changing Both Dimensions

You can write the area of the larger rectangle below as $x(x + 3)$ or $x^2 + 3x$.

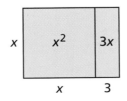

The equation $x(x + 3) = x^2 + 3x$ is an example of the **Distributive Property,** which you studied in earlier units.

The Distributive Property says that, for any three numbers a, b, and c,
$a(b + c) = ab + ac$.

Area:
$a(b + c)$ or $ab + ac$

When you write $a(b + c)$ as $ab + ac$, you are *multiplying*, or writing the expression in expanded form. When you write $ab + ac$ as $a(b + c)$, you are *factoring*, or writing the expression in factored form.

The terms $2x$ and $3x$ are *like terms*. The Distributive Property can be used to add like terms. For example, $2x + 3x = (2 + 3)x = 5x$.

In Problem 2.3, you will explore what happens to the area of a square when both dimensions are changed. You will see how the Distributive Property can be used to change the expression for area from factored form to expanded form.

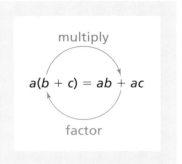

Getting Ready for Problem 2.3

A new rectangle is made by increasing one side of a square with sides of length x by 2 centimeters and increasing the other side by 3 centimeters.

- How do the areas of the square and the new rectangle compare?
- How can you represent the area of the new rectangle?

A. Each rectangle has been subdivided into four smaller rectangles. Write two expressions for the area of the rectangle outlined in red, one in factored form and one in expanded form.

1.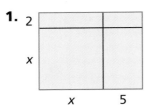

2.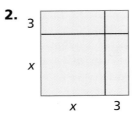

3.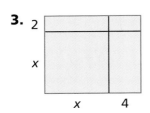

4.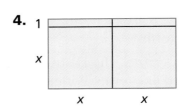

B. A square has sides of length x centimeters. One dimension is doubled and then increased by 2 centimeters. The other dimension is increased by 3 centimeters.

   1. Make a sketch of the new rectangle. Label the area of each section.

   2. Write two expressions, one in factored form and one in expanded form, for the area of the new rectangle.

C. Use a rectangle model to help write each expression in expanded form.

   1. $(x + 3)(x + 5)$ **2.** $(4 + x)(4 + x)$ **3.** $3x(x + 1)$

D. Carminda says she doesn't need a rectangle model to multiply $(x + 3)$ by $(x + 2)$. She uses the Distributive Property.

$$
\begin{aligned}
(x + 3)(x + 2) &= (x + 3)x + (x + 3)2 &&(1)\\
&= x^2 + 3x + 2x + 6 &&(2)\\
&= x^2 + 5x + 6 &&(3)
\end{aligned}
$$

   1. Is Carminda correct? Explain what she did at each step.

   2. Show how using the Distributive Property to multiply $(x + 3)$ and $(x + 5)$ is the same as using a rectangle model.

E. Use the Distributive Property to write each expression in expanded form.

1. $(x + 5)(x + 5)$ **2.** $(x + 3)(x - 4)$ **3.** $2x(5 - x)$

4. $(x - 3)(x - 4)$ **5.** $(x + 2)(x - 2)$

ACE Homework starts on page 30.

2.4 Factoring Quadratic Expressions

You know two ways to change a factored expression, such as $(x + 2)(x + 6)$, to expanded form.

Rectangle Model	Distributive Property

Subdivide.

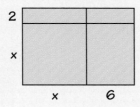

$$(x + 2)(x + 6) = (x + 2)x + (x + 2)6$$

Label areas.

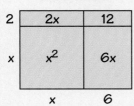

$$= x^2 + 2x + 6x + 12$$

Add the areas of the sections:
$$(x + 2)(x + 6) = x^2 + 2x + 6x + 12$$
$$= x^2 + 8x + 12$$

$$= x^2 + 8x + 12$$

How can you write an expanded expression, such as $x^2 + 8x + 12$, in factored form?

In the next problem, we will use the distributive property to write expressions in factored form.

A. 1. Copy the diagram. Replace each question mark with the correct length or area.

2. Write two expressions for the area of the rectangle outlined in red.

B. Consider this expression.
$$x^2 + bx + 8$$

1. Choose a value for b that gives an expression you can factor. Then, write the expression in factored form.

2. Compare your work with your classmates. Did everyone write the same expressions? Explain.

C. In parts (1)–(4), find values of r and s that make the equations true.

1. $x^2 + 10x + 24 = (x + 6)(x + r)$

2. $x^2 + 11x + 24 = (x + s)(x + r)$

3. $x^2 + 25x + 24 = (x + r)(x + s)$

4. Describe the strategies you used to factor the expressions in parts (1)–(3).

D. Alyse says she can use the Distributive Property to factor the expression $x^2 + 10x + 16$. She writes:

$$x^2 + 10x + 16 = x^2 + 2x + 8x + 16 \qquad (1)$$
$$= x(x + 2) + 8(x + 2) \qquad (2)$$
$$= (x + 2)(x + 8) \qquad (3)$$

Is Alyse correct? Explain what she did at each step.

E. Use the Distributive Property to factor each expression.

1. $x^2 + 5x + 2x + 10$ **2.** $x^2 + 11x + 10$ **3.** $x^2 + 3x - 10$

4. $x^2 + 16x + 15$ **5.** $x^2 - 8x + 15$ **6.** $x^2 - 12x + 36$

ACE Homework starts on page 30.

A Closer Look at Parabolas

In Investigation 1, you saw that graphs of quadratic equations of the form $y = x(a - x)$ are parabolas. A vertical line drawn through the maximum point of a parabola is called a **line of symmetry.** If you were to fold along this line, the two halves of the parabola would exactly match.

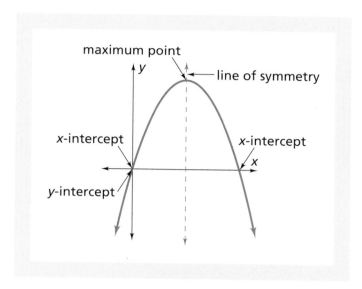

In the last four problems, you worked with expanded and factored forms of quadratic expressions. Next, you will examine graphs of the equations associated with these expressions.

Getting Ready for Problem 2.5

- Sketch the graph of $y = (x + 3)(x - 2)$.
- Describe the features of the graph. Include the x- and y-intercepts, the maximum or minimum point, and the line of symmetry.
- Sketch a graph of $y = x^2 + x - 6$. How does this graph compare with the graph of $y = (x + 3)(x - 2)$? Explain.

In this problem, you will explore these questions:

What can you learn about a quadratic function from its graph?

How are the features of a parabola related to its equation?

Problem 2.5 A Closer Look at Parabolas

These equations, all in factored form, were graphed using the window settings shown at the right. The graphs are shown below.

$y_1 = x^2$

$y_3 = (x + 2)(x + 3)$

$y_5 = x(4 - x)$

$y_7 = x(x + 4)$

$y_2 = 2x(x + 4)$

$y_4 = (x + 3)(x + 3)$

$y_6 = x(x - 4)$

$y_8 = (x + 3)(x - 3)$

WINDOW FORMAT
Xmin=-5
Xmax=5
Xscl=1
Ymin=-10
Ymax=10
Yscl=1
Xres=1

Graph A

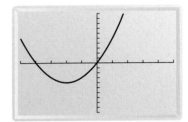

Graph B

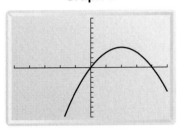

Graph C

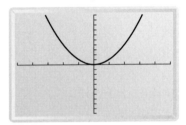

Graph D

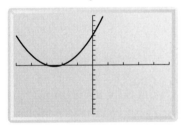

Graph E

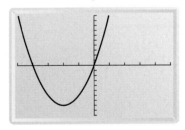

Graph F

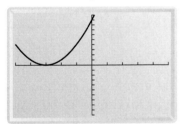

Graph G

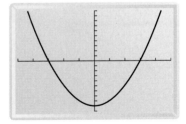

Graph H

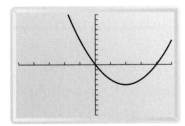

A. Do parts (1)–(5) for each equation.

   1. Match the equation to its graph.

   2. Label the coordinates of the x- and y-intercepts of the graph. Describe how you can predict the x- and y-intercepts from the equation.

   3. Draw the line of symmetry of the graph. Can you predict the location of the line of symmetry from the equation? Explain.

   4. Label the coordinates of the maximum or minimum point. Can you predict the maximum or minimum point from the equation? Explain.

   5. Describe the shape of the graph.

B. **1.** Write each of the equations in expanded form.

   2. What features of the graph can you predict from the expanded form of the equation? What features can you predict from the factored form? Explain.

C. *Without* graphing, describe the graph of each equation. Give as many details as possible.

   1. $y = x^2 + 6x + 5$ **2.** $y = -x^2 + 4x$ **3.** $y = (x - 2)(x + 3)$

D. How can you tell whether an equation represents a quadratic relationship if it is in expanded form? If it is in factored form?

ACE **Homework starts on page 30.**

Applications

1. A square has sides of length x centimeters. One dimension increases by 4 centimeters and the other decreases by 4 centimeters, forming a new rectangle.

   a. Make a table showing the side length and area of the square and the area of the new rectangle. Include whole-number x-values from 4 to 16.

   b. On the same axes, graph the (x, *area*) data for both the square and the rectangle.

   c. Suppose you want to compare the area of a square with the area of the corresponding new rectangle. Is it easier to use the table or the graph?

   d. Write equations for the area of the original square and the area of the new rectangle in terms of x.

   e. Use your calculator to graph both equations. Show values of x from -10 to 10. Copy the graphs onto your paper. Describe the relationship between the two graphs.

2. A square has sides of length x centimeters. One dimension increases by 5 centimeters, forming a new rectangle.

   a. Make a sketch to show the new rectangle.

   b. Write two equations, one in factored form and one in expanded form, for the area of the new rectangle.

   c. Graph the equations in part (b).

For Exercises 3 and 4, draw a divided rectangle whose area is represented by each expression. Label the lengths and area of each section. Then, write an equivalent expression in expanded form.

   3. $x(x + 7)$ **4.** $x(x - 3)$

For Exercises 5–7, draw a divided rectangle whose area is represented by each expression. Label the lengths and area of each section. Then, write an equivalent expression in factored form.

5. $x^2 + 6x$ **6.** $x^2 - 8x$ **7.** $x^2 - x$

For Exercises 8–11, write the expression in factored form.

For: Multiple-Choice Skills Practice
Web Code: apa-4254

8. $x^2 + 10x$ **9.** $x^2 - 6x$

10. $x^2 + 11x$ **11.** $x^2 - 2x$

For Exercises 12–15, write the expression in expanded form.

12. $x(x + 1)$ **13.** $x(x - 10)$

14. $x(x + 6)$ **15.** $x(x - 15)$

For Exercises 16–20, write two expressions, one in factored form and one in expanded form, for the area of the rectangle outlined in red.

16.
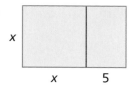

17.
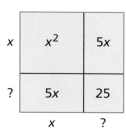

18.
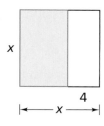

19.
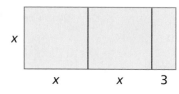

20.
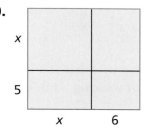

21. A square has sides of length x meters. Both dimensions increase by 5 meters, forming a new square.

   a. Make a sketch to show the new square.

   b. Write two equations, one in factored form and one in expanded form, for the area of the new square in terms of x.

   c. Graph the equations in part (b).

22. A square has sides of length x centimeters. One dimension increases by 4 centimeters and the other increases by 5 centimeters, forming a new rectangle.

 a. Make a sketch to show the new rectangle.

 b. Write two equations, one in factored form and one in expanded form, for the area of the new rectangle.

 c. Graph the equations in part (b).

For Exercises 23–28, use the Distributive Property to write each expression in expanded form.

23. $(x - 3)(x + 4)$ **24.** $(x + 3)(x + 5)$ **25.** $x(x + 5)$

26. $(x - 2)(x - 6)$ **27.** $(x - 3)(x + 3)$ **28.** $(x - 3)(x + 5)$

29. a. Draw and label a rectangle whose area is represented by each expression.

$$x^2 + 3x + 4x + 12 \qquad\qquad x^2 + 7x + 10$$

 b. For each expression in part (a), write an equivalent expression in factored form.

30. Write each expression in factored form.

 a. $x^2 + 13x + 12$ **b.** $x^2 - 13x + 12$ **c.** $x^2 + 8x + 12$

 d. $x^2 - 8x + 12$ **e.** $x^2 + 7x + 12$ **f.** $x^2 - 7x + 12$

 g. $x^2 + 11x - 12$ **h.** $x^2 - 11x - 12$ **i.** $x^2 + 4x - 12$

 j. $x^2 - 4x - 12$ **k.** $x^2 + x - 12$ **l.** $x^2 - x - 12$

Homework Help **O**nline
PHSchool.com

For: Help with Exercise 30
Web Code: ape-4230

For Exercises 31–39, determine whether the equation represents a quadratic relationship *without* making a table or a graph. Explain.

31. $y = 5x + x^2$ **32.** $y = 2x + 8$ **33.** $y = (9 - x)x$

34. $y = 4x(3 + x)$ **35.** $y = 3^x$ **36.** $y = x^2 + 10x$

37. $y = x(x + 4)$ **38.** $y = 2(x + 4)$ **39.** $y = 7x + 10 + x^2$

40. Give the line of symmetry, the x- and y-intercepts, and the maximum or minimum point for the graph of each equation.

   a. $y = (x - 3)(x + 3)$ **b.** $y = x(x + 5)$

   c. $y = (x + 3)(x + 5)$ **d.** $y = (x - 3)(x + 5)$

   e. $y = (x + 3)(x - 5)$

For Exercises 41 and 42, complete parts (a)–(e) for each equation.

41. $y = x^2 + 5x + 6$ **42.** $y = x^2 - 25$

   a. Find an equivalent factored form of the equation.

   b. Identify the x- and y-intercepts for the graph of the equation.

   c. Find the coordinates of the maximum or minimum point.

   d. Find the line of symmetry.

   e. Tell which form of the equation can be used to predict the features in parts (b)–(d) without making a graph.

43. Darnell makes a rectangle from a square by doubling one dimension and adding 3 centimeters. He leaves the other dimension unchanged.

   a. Write an equation for the area A of the new rectangle in terms of the side length x of the original square.

   b. Graph your area equation.

   c. What are the x-intercepts of the graph? How can you find the x-intercepts from the graph? How can you find them from the equation?

For Exercises 44–47, match the equation with its graph. Then, explain how to locate the line of symmetry for the graph.

44. $y = (x + 7)(x + 2)$ **45.** $y = x(x + 3)$

46. $y = (x - 4)(x + 6)$ **47.** $y = (x - 5)(x + 5)$

Graph A

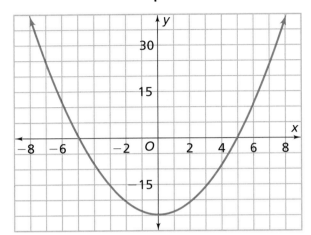

Graph B

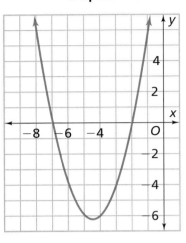

Graph C

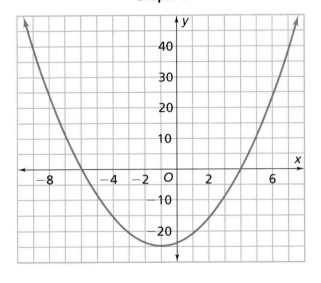

Graph D

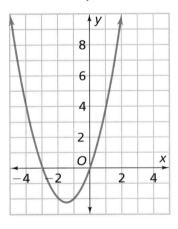

48. a. How are the graphs at the right similar?

  b. How are the graphs different?

  c. The maximum value for $y = x(10 - x)$ occurs when $x = 5$. How can you find the y-coordinate of the maximum value?

  d. The minimum value for $y = x(x - 10)$ occurs when $x = 5$. How can you find the y-coordinate of the minimum value?

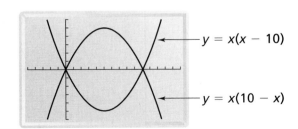

$y = x(x - 10)$

$y = x(10 - x)$

49. Multiple Choice Which quadratic equation has x-intercepts at $(3, 0)$ and $(-1, 0)$?

A. $y = x^2 - 1x + 3$

B. $y = x^2 - 2x + 3$

C. $y = 3x^2 - 1x$

D. $y = x^2 - 2x - 3$

Connections

50. The Stellar International Cellular long-distance company charges $13.95 per month plus $0.39 per minute of calling time. The Call Anytime company charges no monthly service fee but charges $0.95 per minute.

a. Represent each charge plan with an equation, a table, and a graph.

b. For each plan, tell whether the relationship between calling time and monthly cost is quadratic, linear, exponential, or inverse. How do your equation, table, and graph support your answer?

c. For what number of minutes are the costs for the two plans equal?

51. The winner of the Jammin' Jelly jingle contest will receive $500. Antonia and her friends are writing a jingle. They plan to divide the prize money equally if they win.

a. Suppose n friends write the winning jingle. Write an equation to show how much prize money p each of the friends receive.

b. Describe the relationship between the number of friends and the prize money each friend receives.

c. Write a question about this relationship that is easier to answer by using a graph. Write a question that is easier to answer by using a table. Write a question that is easier to answer by using an equation.

d. Is this relationship quadratic, linear, exponential, or inverse? Explain.

52. Suppose the circumference of a cross section of a nearly circular tree is *x* feet.

   a. What is the diameter in terms of *x*?

   b. What is the radius in terms of *x*?

   c. What is the area of the cross section in terms of *x*?

   d. Is the relationship between the circumference *x* and the area of the cross section linear, quadratic, exponential, or none of these?

   e. Suppose the circumference of the cross section is 10 feet. What are the diameter, radius, and area of the cross section?

53. A square has sides of length *x* centimeters.

   a. The square is enlarged by a scale factor of 2. What is the area of the enlarged square?

   b. How does the area of the original square compare with the area of the enlarged square?

   c. Is the new square similar to the original square? Explain.

54. A rectangle has dimensions of *x* centimeters and $(x + 1)$ centimeters.

   a. The rectangle is enlarged by a scale factor of 2. What is the area of the enlarged rectangle?

   b. How does the area of the original rectangle compare with the area of the enlarged rectangle?

   c. Is the new rectangle similar to the original rectangle? Explain.

55. For each polygon, write formulas for the perimeter P and area A in terms of ℓ, if it is possible. If it is not possible to write a formula, explain why.

Rectangle

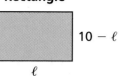
$10 - \ell$
ℓ

Parallelogram

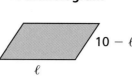
$10 - \ell$
ℓ

Kite

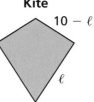
$10 - \ell$
ℓ

Non-isosceles Trapezoid

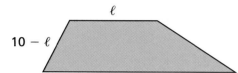
ℓ
$10 - \ell$

Isosceles Right Triangle

ℓ
$10 - \ell$

56. a. Write the equation of the line that passes through the two points shown.

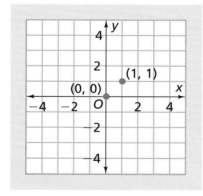

b. Is there a different line that can be drawn through these points? Explain.

For Exercises 57–60, evaluate the expression for the given values of x.

57. $x(x - 5)$ for $x = 5$ and $x = -5$

58. $3x^2 - x$ for $x = 1$ and $x = \frac{1}{3}$

59. $x^2 + 5x + 4$ for $x = 2$ and $x = -4$

60. $(x - 7)(x + 2)$ for $x = -2$ and $x = 2$

Connections

61. Refer to Graphs A, E, and G in Problem 2.5. Without using your calculator, answer the following questions.

  a. Suppose parabola A is shifted 1 unit left. Write an equation for this new parabola.

  b. Suppose parabola E is shifted 4 units right. Write an equation for this new parabola.

  c. Can parabola E be transformed into parabola G by a shift to the right only? Explain.

Extensions

62. Multiple Choice Which expression is equivalent to $(2n + 3)(4n + 2)$?

  F. $8n + 5$ **G.** $6n^2 + 7n + 4n + 5$

  H. $8n^2 + 16n + 6$ **J.** $8n^2 + 6$

For Exercises 63–64, write each expression in factored form. You may want to draw a rectangle model.

63. $2x^2 + 3x + 1$ **64.** $4x^2 + 10x + 6$

65. Sketch graphs of the equations $y = x^2 + 2x$ and $y = x^2 + 2$.

  a. How are the graphs similar?

  b. How are the graphs different?

  c. Find the y-intercept for each graph.

  d. Find the x-intercepts for each graph if they exist. If there are no x-intercepts, explain why.

  e. Do all quadratic relationships have y-intercepts? Explain.

Mathematical Reflections 2

In this investigation, you wrote quadratic expressions to represent areas of rectangles formed by transforming a square. You converted expressions to different forms by using rectangular models and by using the Distributive Property. These questions will help you summarize what you have learned.

Think about your answers to these questions. Discuss your ideas with other students and your teacher. Then, write a summary of your findings in your notebook.

1. Show how the area of a rectangle can illustrate the Distributive Property.

2. Explain how you can use the Distributive Property to answer each question. Use examples to help with your explanations.

   a. Suppose a quadratic expression is in factored form. How can you find an equivalent expression in expanded form?

   b. Suppose a quadratic expression is in expanded form. How can you find an equivalent expression in factored form?

3. How can you recognize a quadratic function from its equation?

4. Describe what you know about the shape of the graph of a quadratic function. Include important features of the graph and describe how you can predict these features from its equation.

Quadratic Patterns of Change

In previous units, you studied patterns in linear and exponential relationships. In this investigation, you will look for patterns in quadratic relationships as you solve some interesting counting problems.

What patterns of change characterize linear and exponential relationships?

What patterns of change did you notice in the quadratic relationships in Investigations 1 and 2?

3.1 Exploring Triangular Numbers

Study the pattern of dots.

Figure 1   **Figure 2**   **Figure 3**   **Figure 4**

How many dots do you predict will be in Figure 5? In Figure n*?*

The numbers that represent the number of dots in each triangle above are called **triangular numbers.** The first triangular number is 1, the second triangular number is 3, the third is 6, the fourth is 10, and so on.

You can also represent triangular numbers with patterns of squares.
The number of squares in Figure n is the nth triangular number.

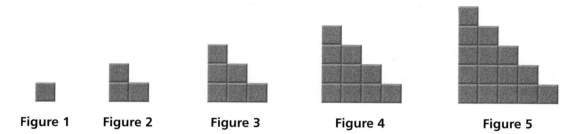

Figure 1   **Figure 2**   **Figure 3**   **Figure 4**   **Figure 5**

A. 1. What is the sixth triangular number? What is the tenth triangular number?

   2. Make a table of (*figure number, triangular number*) values for the first ten triangular numbers.

   3. Describe the pattern of change from one triangular number to the next.

   4. Describe how you can use the pattern in the table to find the 11th and 12th triangular numbers.

B. 1. Write an equation for the nth triangular number t. In other words, write an equation for the number of squares t in Figure n. Explain your reasoning.

   2. Use your equation to find the 11th and 12th triangular numbers.

C. 1. Use a calculator to graph your equation. Show n values from -5 to 5. Make a sketch of your graph.

   2. Does your graph represent the relationship you observed in the table? Explain.

   3. Does your equation represent a quadratic relationship? Explain.

   4. Compare this equation with the equations in Investigations 1 and 2.

ACE **Homework starts on page 44.**

3.2 Counting Handshakes

After a sporting event, the opposing teams often line up and shake hands. To celebrate their victory, members of the winning team may congratulate each other with a round of high fives.

Problem 3.2 Another Quadratic Relationship

Consider three cases of handshaking:

Case 1 Two teams have the same number of players. Each player on one team shakes hands with each player on the other team.

Case 2 One team has one more player than the other. Each player on one team shakes hands with each player on the other team.

Case 3 Each member of a team gives a high five to each teammate.

A. Consider Case 1.

    1. How many handshakes will take place between two 5-player teams? Between two 10-player teams?

    2. Write an equation for the number of handshakes h between two n-player teams.

B. Consider Case 2.

    1. How many handshakes will take place between a 6-player team and a 7-player team? Between an 8-player team and a 9-player team?

    2. Write an equation for the number of handshakes h between an n-player team and an $(n - 1)$-player team.

C. Consider Case 3.

    1. How many high fives will take place among a team with 4 members? Among a team with 8 members?

    2. Write an equation for the number of high fives h among a team with n members.

ACE Homework starts on page 44.

3.3 Examining Patterns of Change

In this problem, you will examine the patterns of change that characterize quadratic relationships.

Problem 3.3 Examining Patterns of Change

    A. Complete parts (1)–(2) for each case in Problem 3.2.

        1. Make a table showing the number of players on each team and the number of handshakes or high fives. Include data for teams with 1 to 10 members.

        2. Describe a pattern of change that can help you predict the numbers of handshakes or high fives for larger teams.

    B. Compare the patterns in the three tables you made in Question A. How are the patterns similar? How are they different?

    C. 1. Use your calculator to graph the equations you wrote for the three cases in Problem 3.2. Show n values from -10 to 10. Make a sketch of the graph.

        2. Compare the three graphs.

    D. For each case, compare the table and its graph. Describe how the tables and graphs show the same pattern of change.

    E. Are any of the three relationships quadratic? Explain.

    F. Compare the patterns of change for the three cases with the patterns of change you observed in Investigations 1 and 2.

ACE Homework starts on page 44.

Applications

1. These dot patterns represent the first four *square numbers*, 1, 4, 9, and 16.

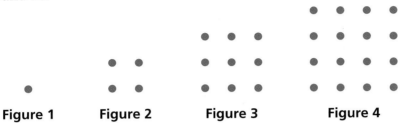

| Figure 1 | Figure 2 | Figure 3 | Figure 4 |

   a. What are the next two square numbers?

   b. Write an equation for the *n*th square number *s*.

   c. Make a table and a graph of (n, s) values for the first ten square numbers. Describe the pattern of change from one square number to the next.

2. The numbers of dots in the figures below are the first four *rectangular numbers*.

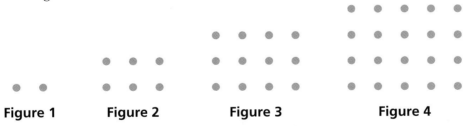

| Figure 1 | Figure 2 | Figure 3 | Figure 4 |

   a. What are the first four rectangular numbers?

   b. Find the next two rectangular numbers.

   c. Describe the pattern of change from one rectangular number to the next.

   d. Predict the 7th and 8th rectangular numbers.

   e. Write an equation for the *n*th rectangular number *r*.

3. In Problem 3.1, you looked at triangular numbers.

   a. What is the 18th triangular number?

   b. Is 210 a triangular number? Explain.

4. a. In Problem 3.1, you found an equation for the *n*th triangular number. Sam claims he can use this equation to find the sum of the first 10 counting numbers. Explain why Sam is correct.

    b. What is the sum of the first 10 counting numbers?

    c. What is the sum of the first 15 counting numbers?

    d. What is the sum of the first *n* counting numbers?

Did You Know?

Carl Friedrich Gauss (1777–1855) was a German mathematician and astronomer. When Gauss was about eight years old, his teacher asked his class to find the sum of the first 100 counting numbers. Gauss had the answer almost immediately!

Gauss realized that he could pair up the numbers as shown. Each pair has a sum of 101.

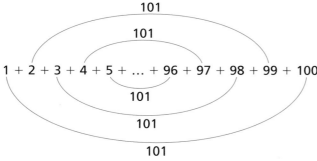

There are 100 numbers, so there are 50 pairs. This means the sum is $50 \times 101 = 5{,}050$ [or $\frac{100}{2}(101)$ or $\frac{100}{2}$ (first number plus last number)].

Go Online
PHSchool.com
For: Information about Gauss
Web Code: ape-9031

For Exercises 5–8, tell whether the number is a triangular number, a square number, a rectangular number, or none of these. Explain.

    5. 110   **6.** 66   **7.** 121   **8.** 60

9. In a middle school math league, each team has six student members and two coaches.

Johnson
Middle School

Hillsdale
Middle School

  a. At the start of a match, the coaches and student members of one team exchange handshakes with the coaches and student members of the other team. How many handshakes occur?

  b. At the end of the match, the members and coaches of the winning team exchange handshakes. How many handshakes occur?

  c. The members of one team exchange handshakes with their coaches. How many handshakes occur?

10. In a 100-meter race, five runners are from the United States and three runners are from Canada.

  a. How many handshakes occur if the runners from one country exchange handshakes with the runners from the other country?

  b. How many high fives occur if the runners from the United States exchange high fives?

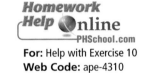

Homework Help Online PHSchool.com
For: Help with Exercise 10
Web Code: ape-4310

11. A company rents five offices in a building. There is a cable connecting each pair of offices.

  a. How many cables are there in all?

  b. Suppose the company rents two more offices. How many cables will they need in all?

  c. Compare this situation with Case 3 in Problem 3.2.

For Exercises 12–15, describe a situation that can be represented by the equation. Tell what the variables p and n represent in that situation.

12. $p = n(n - 1)$ **13.** $p = 2n$

14. $p = n(n - 2)$ **15.** $p = n(16 - n)$

16. The graphs below represent equations for situations you have looked at in this unit.

Graph I

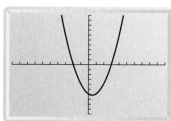

Graph II

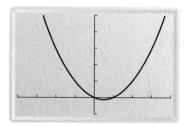

Graph III

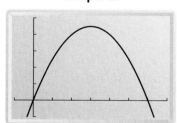

Graph IV

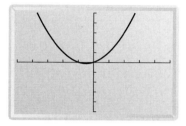

a. Which graph might represent the equation for the number of high fives exchanged among a team with n players? Explain.

b. Which graph might represent the equation for the areas of rectangles with a fixed perimeter?

c. Which graph might represent the equation for the areas of a rectangle formed by increasing one dimension of a square by 2 centimeters and decreasing the other dimension by 3 centimeters?

d. Which graph might represent the equation for a triangular-number pattern?

For Exercises 17–19, the tables represent quadratic relationships. Copy and complete each table.

17.

x	y
0	0
1	1
2	3
3	6
4	■
5	■
6	■

18.

x	y
0	0
1	3
2	8
3	15
4	■
5	■
6	■

19.

x	y
0	0
1	4
2	6
3	6
4	■
5	■
6	■

Connections

20. **a.** Make sketches that show two ways of completing the rectangle model at the right using whole numbers. For each sketch, express the area of the largest rectangle in both expanded form and factored form.

    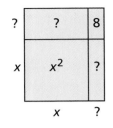

    b. Is there more than one way to complete the rectangle model below using whole numbers? Explain.

    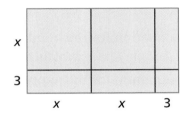

21. Write two equivalent expressions for the area of the rectangle outlined in red below.

22. Consider these quadratic expressions.

    $$2x^2 + 7x + 6 \qquad x^2 + 6x + 8$$

    a. For each expression, sketch a rectangle whose area the expression represents.

    b. Write each expression in factored form. Which expression is easier to factor? Why?

For Exercises 23–28, write the expression in expanded form.

29 $x(5 - x)$

24. $(x + 1)(x + 3)$

25. $(x - 1)(x + 3)$

26. $3x(x + 5)$

27. $(2x + 1)(x + 3)$

28. $(2x - 1)(x + 3)$

For Exercises 29–35, write the expression in factored form.

29. $x^2 - 9x + 8$

30. $4x^2 - 6x$

31. $x^2 - 2x - 3$

32. $3x^2 + 14x + 8$

33. $4x^2 + 6x$

34. $4x^2 - x - 3$

35. $x^3 - 2x^2 - 3x$

Go Online
PHSchool.com

For: Multiple-Choice Skills Practice
Web Code: apa-4354

36. Min was having trouble factoring the expression in Exercise 32. Ricardo suggested that she use a rectangle model.

   a. Explain how a rectangle model can help Min factor the expression. Make a sketch to illustrate your explanation.

   b. How can you factor this expression without drawing a rectangle?

37. A diagonal of a polygon is a line segment connecting any two nonadjacent vertices. A quadrilateral has two diagonals like the one at the right.

   a. How many diagonals does a pentagon have? How many does a hexagon have? A heptagon? An octagon?

   b. How many diagonals does an *n*-sided polygon have?

38. These "trains" are formed by joining identical squares.

Train 1   Train 2   Train 3   Train 4   Train 5

   a. How many rectangles are in each of the first five trains? For example, the drawing below shows the six rectangles in Train 3. (Remember, a square is a rectangle.)

   b. Make a table showing the number of rectangles in each of the first ten trains.

   c. How can you use the pattern of change in your table to find the number of rectangles in Train 15?

   d. Write an equation for the number of rectangles in Train *n*.

   e. Use your equation to find the number of rectangles in Train 15.

39. a. What is the area of the base of the can?

b. How many centimeter cubes or parts of cubes can fit in a single layer on the bottom of the can?

c. How many layers of this size would fill the can?

d. Use your answers to parts (a)–(c) to find the volume of the can.

e. The label on the lateral surface of the can is a rectangle with a height of 10 cm. What is the other dimension of the label?

f. What is the area of the label?

g. Use your answers to parts (a) and (f) to find the surface area of the can.

10 cm

10 cm

40. A company is trying to choose a box shape for a new product. It has narrowed the choices to the triangular prism and the cylinder shown below.

4 cm

5 cm

3 cm

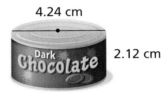

4.24 cm

2.12 cm

a. Sketch a net for each box.

b. Find the surface area of each box.

c. Which box will require more cardboard to construct?

For Exercise 41–44, tell whether the pattern in the table is linear, quadratic, exponential, or none of these.

41.

x	y
0	2
3	4
5	5
6	6
7	7
8	8
10	10

42.

x	y
−3	12
−2	7
−1	4
0	3
1	4
2	7
3	12

43.

x	y
0	1
2	9
5	243
6	729
7	2,187
8	6,561
10	59,049

44.

x	y
1	−2
2	0
3	3
4	8
5	15
6	24
7	14

45. Multiple Choice Which equation represents a quadratic relationship?

A. $y = (x - 1)(6 - 2)$ **B.** $y = 2x(3 - 2)$

C. $y = 2^x$ **D.** $y = x(x + 2)$

46. Multiple Choice Which equation has a graph with a minimum point at $(1, 4)$?

F. $y = -x^2 + 5$ **G.** $y = -x^2 + 5x$

H. $y = x^2 - 2x + 5$ **J.** $y = -x^2 + 7x - 10$

Extensions

47. You can use Gauss's method to find the sum of the whole numbers from 1 to 10 by writing the sum twice as shown and adding vertically.

$$1 + 2 + 3 + 4 + 5 + 6 + 7 + 8 + 9 + 10$$
$$\underline{10 + 9 + 8 + 7 + 6 + 5 + 4 + 3 + 2 + 1}$$
$$11 + 11 + 11 + 11 + 11 + 11 + 11 + 11 + 11 + 11$$

Each vertical sum of 11 occurs 10 times, or $10(11) = 110$. This result is twice the sum of the numbers from 1 to 10, so we divide by 2 to get $\frac{10(11)}{2} = \frac{110}{2} = 55$.

a. How can you use this idea to find $1 + 2 + 3 + \ldots + 99 + 100$?

b. How could you use this idea to find $1 + 2 + 3 + \ldots + n$ for any whole number n?

c. How is this method related to Gauss's method?

48. The patterns of dots below represent the first three *star numbers*.

Figure 1   **Figure 2**   **Figure 3**

    a. What are the first three star numbers?

    b. Find the next three star numbers.

    c. Write an equation you could use to calculate the *n*th star number.

49. In parts (a) and (b), explain your answers by drawing pictures or writing a convincing argument.

    a. Ten former classmates attend their class reunion. They all shake hands with each other. How many handshakes occur?

    b. A little later, two more classmates arrive. Suppose these two people shake hands with each other and the ten other classmates. How many new handshakes occur?

50. The pattern of dots below represents the first three *hexagonal numbers*.

Figure 1　　　**Figure 2**　　　**Figure 3**

    a. What are the first three hexagonal numbers?

    b. Find the next two hexagonal numbers.

    c. Write an equation you can use to calculate the nth hexagonal number.

51. There are 30 squares of various sizes in this 4-by-4 grid.

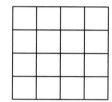

    a. Sixteen of the squares are the identical small squares that make up the grid. Find the other 14 squares. Draw pictures or give a description.

    b. How many squares are in an n-by-n grid? (**Hint:** Start with some simple cases and search for a pattern.)

Mathematical Reflections 3

In this investigation, you counted handshakes and studied geometric patterns. You found that these situations can be represented by quadratic functions. These questions will help you summarize what you have learned.

Think about your answers to these questions. Discuss your ideas with other students and your teacher. Then, write a summary of your findings in your notebook.

1. a. In what ways is the triangle-number relationship similar to the relationships in the handshake problems? In what ways are these relationships different?

   b. In what ways are the quadratic functions in this investigation similar to the quadratic functions in Investigations 1 and 2? In what ways are they different?

2. a. In a table of values for a quadratic function, how can you use the pattern of change to predict the next value?

   b. How can you use a table of values to decide if a function is quadratic?

What Is a Quadratic Function?

When you jump from a diving board, gravity pulls you toward Earth. When you throw or kick a ball into the air, gravity brings it back down. For several hundred years, scientists have used mathematical models to describe and predict the effect of gravity on the position, velocity, and acceleration of falling objects.

Did You Know?

Aristotle, the ancient Greek philosopher and scientist, believed that heavier objects fall faster than lighter objects. In the late 1500s, the great Italian scientist Galileo challenged this idea.

It is said that, while observing a hailstorm, Galileo noticed that large and small hailstones hit the ground at the same time. If Aristotle were correct, this would happen only if the larger stones dropped from a higher point or if the smaller stones started falling first. Galileo didn't think either of these explanations was probable.

A famous story claims that Galileo proved that heavy and light objects fall at the same rate by climbing to the highest point he could find—the top of the Tower of Pisa—and dropping two objects simultaneously. Although they had different weights, the objects hit the ground at the same time.

Go Online
PHSchool.com **For:** Information about Galileo **Web Code:** ape-9031

4.1 Tracking a Ball

No matter how hard you throw or kick a ball into the air, gravity returns it to Earth. In this problem, you will explore how the height of a thrown ball changes over time.

Problem 4.1 Interpreting a Table and an Equation

Suppose you throw a ball straight up in the air. This table shows how the height of the ball might change as it goes up and then returns to the ground.

A. 1. Describe how the height of the ball changes over this 4-second time period.

   2. Without actually making the graph, describe what the graph of these data would look like. Include as many important features as you can.

   3. Do you think these data represent a quadratic function? Explain.

B. The height h of the ball in feet after t seconds can be described by the equation $h = -16t^2 + 64t$.

   1. Graph this equation on your calculator.

   2. Does the graph match the description you gave in Question A? Explain.

   3. When does the ball reach a height of about 58 feet? Explain.

   4. Use the equation to find the height of the ball after 1.6 seconds.

   5. When will the ball reach the ground? Explain.

ACE Homework starts on page 64.

Height of Thrown Ball

Time (seconds)	Height (feet)
0.00	0
0.25	15
0.50	28
0.75	39
1.00	48
1.25	55
1.50	60
1.75	63
2.00	64
2.25	63
2.50	60
2.75	55
3.00	48
3.25	39
3.50	28
3.75	15
4.00	0

Many animals are known for their jumping abilities. Most frogs can jump several times their body length. Fleas are tiny, but they can easily leap onto a dog or a cat. Some humans have amazing jumping ability as well. Many professional basketball players have vertical leaps of more than 3 feet!

Getting Ready for Problem

In Problem 4.1, the initial height of the ball is 0 feet. This is not very realistic because it means you would have to lie on the ground and release the ball without extending your arm. A more realistic equation for the height of the ball is $h = -16t^2 + 64t + 6$.

- Compare this equation with the equation in Problem 4.1.
- Use your calculator to make a table and a graph of this quadratic function.
- Compare your graph with the graph of the equation in Problem 4.1. Consider the following:
  - the maximum height reached by the ball
  - the x-intercepts
  - the y-intercepts
  - the patterns of change in the height of the ball over time

A. Suppose a frog, a flea, and a basketball player jump straight up. Their heights in feet after t seconds are modeled by these equations.

Frog: $h = -16t^2 + 12t + 0.2$

Flea: $h = -16t^2 + 8t$

Basketball player: $h = -16t^2 + 16t + 6.5$

1. Use your calculator to make tables and graphs of these three equations. Look at heights for time values between 0 seconds and 1 second. In your tables, use time intervals of 0.1 second.

2. What is the maximum height reached by each jumper? When is the maximum height reached?

3. How long does each jump last?

4. What do the constant terms 0.2 and 6.5 tell you about the frog and the basketball player? How is this information represented on the graph?

5. For each jumper, describe the pattern of change in the height over time. Explain how the pattern is reflected in the table and the graph.

B. A jewelry maker would like to increase his profit by raising the price of his jade earrings. However, he knows that if he raises the price too high, he won't sell as many earrings and his profit will decrease.

The jewelry maker's business consultant develops the equation $P = 50s - s^2$ to predict the monthly profit P for a sales price s.

1. Make a table and a graph for this equation.

2. What do the equation, table, and graph suggest about the relationship between sales price and profit?

3. What sales price will bring the greatest profit?

4. How does this equation compare with the equations in Question A? How does it compare with other equations in this unit?

ACE Homework starts on page 64.

- The average flea weighs 0.000001 pound and is 2 to 3 millimeters long. It can pull 160,000 times its own weight and can jump 150 times its own length. This is equivalent to a human being pulling 24 million pounds and jumping nearly 1,000 feet!

- There are 3,000 known species and subspecies of fleas. Fleas are found on all land masses, including Antarctica.

- Most fleas make their homes on bats, rats, squirrels, and mice.

- The bubonic plague, which killed a quarter of Europe's population in the fourteenth century, was spread by rat fleas.

- Flea circuses originated about 300 years ago and were popular in the United States a century ago.

Go Online
PHSchool.com   **For:** Information about fleas
Web Code: ape-9031

4.3 Putting It All Together

You have used equations to model a variety of quadratic functions. You may have noticed some common characteristics of these equations. You have also observed patterns in the graphs and tables of quadratic functions.

To understand a relationship, it helps to look at how the value of one variable changes each time the value of the other variable increases by a fixed amount. For a linear relationship, the y-value increases by a constant amount each time the x-value increases by 1.

Look at this table for the linear relationship $y = 3x + 1$. The "first differences" are the differences between consecutive y-values.

Because the y-value increases by 3 each time the x-value increases by 1, the first differences for $y = 3x + 1$ are all 3.

Now, you'll look at differences for quadratic relationships.

$y = 3x + 1$

x	y
0	1
1	4
2	7
3	10
4	13
5	16

First differences

$4 - 1 = 3$
$7 - 4 = 3$
$10 - 7 = 3$
$13 - 10 = 3$
$16 - 13 = 3$

Getting Ready for Problem 4.3

The simplest quadratic relationship is $y = x^2$, and it is the rule for generating square numbers. In fact, the word *quadratic* comes from the Latin word for "square."

The table below shows that the first differences for $y = x^2$ are not constant.

$y = x^2$

x	y
0	0
1	1
2	4
3	9
4	16
5	25

First differences

$1 - 0 = 1$
$4 - 1 = 3$
$9 - 4 = 5$
$16 - 9 = 7$
$25 - 16 = 9$

- What happens when you look at the "second differences" for $y = x^2$?

$y = x^2$

x	y
0	0
1	1
2	4
3	9
4	16
5	25

First differences

$1 - 0 = 1$
$4 - 1 = 3$
$9 - 4 = 5$
$16 - 9 = 7$
$25 - 16 = 9$

Second differences

$3 - 1 = 2$
$5 - 3 = 2$
$7 - 5 = 2$
$9 - 7 = 2$

- Study the pattern of first and second differences for $y = x^2$. Do you think the tables for other quadratic functions will show a similar pattern?

Problem 4.3 Functions and Patterns of Change

A. **1.** Make a table of values for each quadratic equation below. Include integer values of x from -5 to 5. Show the first and second differences as is done for the table above.

   a. $y = 2x(x + 3)$ **b.** $y = 3x - x^2$

   c. $y = (x - 2)^2$ **d.** $y = x^2 + 5x + 6$

   2. Consider the patterns of change in the values of y and in the first and second differences. In what ways are the patterns similar for the four tables? In what ways are they different?

   3. What patterns of change seem to occur for quadratic relationships?

B. **1.** Make a table of (x, y) values for each equation below. Show the first and second differences.

   a. $y = x + 2$ **b.** $y = 2x$ **c.** $y = 2^x$ **d.** $y = x^2$

   2. Consider the patterns of change in the values of y and in the first and second differences. How are the patterns similar in all four tables? How are they different?

   3. How can you use the patterns of change in tables to identify the type of relationship?

ACE Homework starts on page 64.

Leon invents a puzzle. He makes a large cube from 1,000 centimeter cubes. He paints the faces of the large cube. When the paint dries, he separates the puzzle into the original centimeter cubes. The object of Leon's puzzle is to reassemble the cubes so that no unpainted faces are showing.

When Leon examines the centimeter cubes, he notices that some are painted on only one face, some on two faces, and some on three faces. Many aren't painted at all.

active math
online

For: Painted Cubes Activity
Visit: PHSchool.com
Web Code: apd-4401

Problem 4.4 Looking at Several Functions

In this problem, you will investigate smaller versions of Leon's puzzle.

A. 1. The cube at the right is made of centimeter cubes. The faces of this cube are painted. Suppose you broke the cube into centimeter cubes. How many centimeter cubes would be painted on

   a. three faces?

   b. two faces?

   c. one face?

   d. no faces?

2. Answer the questions from part (1) for cubes with edges with lengths of 3, 4, 5, and 6 centimeters.

Organize your data in a table like the one below.

Edge Length of Large Cube	Number of Centimeter Cubes	Number of Centimeter Cubes Painted On			
		3 faces	2 faces	1 face	0 faces
2					
3					
4					
5					
6					

B. Study the patterns in the table.

   1. Describe the relationship between the edge length of the large cube and the total number of centimeter cubes.

   2. Describe the relationship between the edge length of the large cube and the number of centimeter cubes painted on

   a. three faces   **b.** two faces

   c. one face   **d.** zero faces

   3. Decide whether each relationship in parts (1) and (2) is linear, quadratic, exponential, or none of these.

C. 1. Write an equation for each relationship in parts (1) and (2) of Question B. Tell what the variables and numbers in each equation mean.

   2. Sketch the graph of each equation. What shapes could you have predicted? Explain.

ACE Homework starts on page 64.

Applications

1. A signal flare is fired into the air from a boat. The height h of the flare in feet after t seconds is $h = -16t^2 + 160t$.

    a. How high will the flare travel? When will it reach this maximum height?

    b. When will the flare hit the water?

    c. Explain how you could use a table and a graph to answer the questions in parts (a) and (b).

2. A model rocket is launched from the top of a hill. The table shows how the rocket's height above ground level changes as it travels through the air.

    a. How high above ground level does the rocket travel? When does it reach this maximum height?

    b. From what height is the rocket launched?

    c. How long does it take the rocket to return to the top of the hill?

Height of Model Rocket

Time (seconds)	Height (feet)
0.00	84
0.25	99
0.50	112
0.75	123
1.00	132
1.25	139
1.50	144
1.75	147
2.00	148
2.25	147
2.50	144
2.75	139
3.00	132
3.25	123
3.50	112
3.75	99
4.00	84

3. A basketball player takes a shot. The graph shows the height of the ball, starting when it leaves the player's hands.

a. Estimate the height of the ball when the player releases it.

b. When does the ball reach its maximum height? What is the maximum height?

c. How long does it take the ball to reach the basket (a height of 10 feet)?

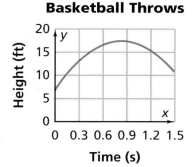

Basketball Throws

4. The highest dive in the Olympic Games is from a 10-meter platform. The height h in meters of a diver t seconds after leaving the platform can be estimated by the equation $h = 10 + 4.9t - 4.9t^2$.

Homework Help Online
PHSchool.com
For: Help with Exercise 4
Web Code: ape-4404

a. Make a table of the relationship between time and height.

b. Sketch a graph of the relationship between time and height.

c. When will the diver hit the water's surface? How can you find this answer by using your graph? How can you find this answer by using your table?

d. When will the diver be 5 meters above the water?

e. When is the diver falling at the fastest rate? How is this shown in the table? How is this shown in the graph?

5. Kelsey jumps from a diving board, springing up into the air and then dropping feet-first. The distance d in feet from her feet to the pool's surface t seconds after she jumps is $d = -16t^2 + 18t + 10$.

a. What is the maximum height of Kelsey's feet during this jump? When does the maximum height occur?

b. When do Kelsey's feet hit the water?

c. What does the constant term 10 in the equation tell you about Kelsey's jump?

6. The equation $h = -16t^2 + 48t + 8$ describes how the height h of a ball in feet changes over time t.

  a. What is the maximum height reached by the ball? Explain how you could use a table and a graph to find the answer.

  b. When does the ball hit the ground? Explain how you could use a table and a graph to find the answer.

  c. Describe the pattern of change in the height of the ball over time. Explain how this pattern would appear in a table and a graph.

  d. What does the constant term 8 mean in this context?

For Exercises 7–10, do parts (a)–(d) without a calculator.

  a. Sketch a graph of the equation.

  b. Find the x- and y-intercepts. Label these points on your graph.

  c. Draw and label the line of symmetry.

  d. Label the coordinates of the maximum or minimum point.

7. $y = 9 - x^2$ **8.** $y = 2x^2 - 4x$

9. $y = 6x - x^2$ **10.** $y = x^2 + 6x + 8$

11. a. How can you tell from a quadratic equation whether the graph will have a maximum point or a minimum point?

  b. How are the x- and y-intercepts of the graph of a quadratic function related to its equation?

  c. How are the x- and y-intercepts related to the line of symmetry?

For Exercises 12–17, predict the shape of the graph of the equation. Give the maximum or minimum point, the x-intercepts, and the line of symmetry. Use a graphing calculator to check your predictions.

12. $y = x^2$ **13.** $y = -x^2$ **14.** $y = x^2 + 1$

15. $y = x^2 + 6x + 9$ **16.** $y = x^2 - 2$ **17.** $y = x(4 - x)$

For Exercises 18–22, tell whether the table represents a quadratic relationship. If it does, tell whether the relationship has a maximum value or a minimum value.

Go Online
PHSchool.com
For: Multiple-Choice Skills Practice
Web Code: apa-4454

18.

x	−3	−2	−1	0	1	2	3	4	5
y	−4	1	4	5	4	1	−4	−11	−18

19.

x	0	1	2	3	4	5	6	7	8
y	2	3	6	11	18	27	38	51	66

20.

x	0	1	2	3	4	5	6	7	8
y	0	−4	−6	−6	−4	0	6	14	24

21.

x	−4	−3	−2	−1	0	1	2	3	4
y	5	4	3	2	1	2	3	4	5

22.

x	−4	−3	−2	−1	0	1	2	3	4
y	18	10	4	0	−2	−2	0	4	10

23. a. For each equation, investigate the pattern of change in the *y*-values. Describe the patterns you find.

$$y = 2x^2 \qquad y = 3x^2 \qquad y = \tfrac{1}{2}x^2 \qquad y = -2x^2$$

b. Use what you discovered in part (a) to predict the pattern of change for each of these equations.

$$y = 5x^2 \qquad y = -4x^2 \qquad y = \tfrac{1}{4}x^2 \qquad y = ax^2$$

c. Do your observations hold for $y = 2x^2 + 5$? Do they hold for $y = 2x^2 + 5x$?

24. a. Make a table of (x, y) values for the six points shown on the graph.

b. The graph shows a quadratic relationship. Extend the graph to show *x*-values from 5 to 10. Explain how you know your graph is correct.

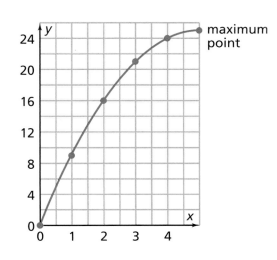

maximum point

25. The graph shows a quadratic relationship. Extend the graph to show x-values from -4 to 0.

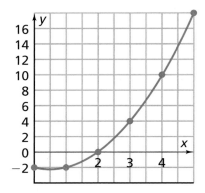

26. The table at the right shows a quadratic relationship. Extend the table to show x-values from 0 to -5. Explain how you know your table is correct.

x	y
0	8
1	3
2	0
3	−1
4	0
5	3

27. A cube with edges of length 12 centimeters is built from centimeter cubes. The faces of the large cube are painted. How many centimeter cubes will have

a. three painted faces? **b.** two painted faces?

c. one painted face? **d.** no painted faces?

28. Four large cubes are built from centimeter cubes. The faces of each large cube are painted. In parts (a)–(d), determine the size of the large cube.

a. For Cube A, 1,000 of the centimeter cubes have no painted faces.

b. For Cube B, 864 of the centimeter cubes have one painted face.

c. For Cube C, 132 of the centimeter cubes have two painted faces.

d. For Cube D, 8 of the centimeter cubes have three painted faces.

29. a. Copy and complete each table. Describe the pattern of change.

x	x
1	▧
2	▧
3	▧
4	▧
5	▧

x	x^2
1	▧
2	▧
3	▧
4	▧
5	▧

x	x^3
1	▧
2	▧
3	▧
4	▧
5	▧

b. For each table, tell which column in the painted-cubes table in Problem 4.4 has a similar pattern. Explain.

30. Consider the relationships described by these equations. Are any of them similar to relationships in the painted-cubes situation? Explain.

$$y_1 = 2(x - 1) \qquad y_2 = (x - 1)^3 \qquad y_3 = 4(x - 1)^2$$

Connections

31. a. Describe the patterns of change in each table. (Look closely. You may find more than one.) Explain how you can use the patterns to find the missing entry.

Table 1

x	y
0	25
1	50
2	100
3	200
4	400
5	▨

Table 2

x	y
−3	3
−2	6
−1	9
0	12
1	15
2	▨

Table 3

x	y
2	6
3	12
4	20
5	30
6	42
7	▨

Table 4

x	y
−2	21
−1	24
0	25
1	24
2	21
3	▨

b. Tell which equation matches each table.

$$y_1 = x^2 - 12 \qquad\qquad y_2 = x(x + 1) \qquad\qquad y_3 = 25 - x^2$$
$$y_4 = (x)(x)(x) \qquad\qquad y_5 = 3(x + 4) \qquad\qquad y_6 = 25(2)^x$$

c. Which tables represent quadratic functions? Explain.

d. Do any of the tables include the maximum y-value for the relationship?

e. Do any of the tables include the minimum y-value for the relationship?

32. A potter wants to increase her profits by changing the price of a particular style of vase. Using past sales data, she writes these two equations relating income I to selling price p:

$$I = (100 - p)p \text{ and } I = 100p - p^2$$

a. Are the two equations equivalent? Explain.

b. Show that $I = 100 - p^2$ is not equivalent to the original equations.

c. It costs \$350 to rent a booth at a craft fair. The potter's profit for the fair will be her income minus the cost of the booth. Write an equation for the profit M as a function of the price p.

d. What price would give the maximum profit? What will the maximum profit be?

e. For what prices will there be a profit rather than a loss?

33. A square has sides of length x.

a. Write formulas for the area A and perimeter P of the square in terms of x.

b. Suppose the side lengths of the square are doubled. How do the area and perimeter change?

c. How do the area and perimeter change if the side lengths are tripled?

d. What is the perimeter of a square if its area is 36 square meters?

e. Make a table of side length, perimeter, and area values for squares with whole-number side lengths from 0 to 12.

f. Sketch graphs of the (*side length, area*) and (*side length, perimeter*) data from your table.

g. Tell whether the patterns of change in the tables and graphs suggest linear, quadratic, exponential relationships, or none of these. Explain.

34. Eggs are often sold by the dozen. When farmers send eggs to supermarkets, they often stack the eggs in bigger containers in blocks of 12 eggs × 12 eggs × 12 eggs.

a. How many eggs are in each layer of the container?

b. How many eggs are there in an entire container?

35. A cube has edges of length x.

   a. Write a formula for the volume V of the cube in terms of x.

   b. Suppose the edge lengths of the cube double. How does the volume change?

   c. How do the surface area and volume change if the edge lengths triple?

   d. Make a table for cubes with whole number edge lengths from 0 to 12. Title the columns "Side Length," "Surface Area," and "Volume."

   e. Sketch graphs of the (*edge length, surface area*) and (*edge length, volume*) data from your table.

   f. Tell whether the patterns of change in the tables and graphs suggest linear, quadratic, exponential relationships, or none of these.

36. Write each expression in expanded form.

   a. $-3x(2x - 1)$ **b.** $1.5x(6 - 2x)$

37. Write each expression in expanded form. Look for a pattern. Make a generalization about the expanded form of expressions of the form $(x + a)(x + a)$.

   a. $(x + 1)(x + 1)$ **b.** $(x + 5)(x + 5)$ **c.** $(x - 5)(x - 5)$

38. Write each expression in expanded form. Look for a pattern. Make a generalization about the expanded form of expressions of the form $(x + a)(x - a)$.

   a. $(x + 1)(x - 1)$ **b.** $(x + 5)(x - 5)$ **c.** $(x + 1.5)(x - 1.5)$

39. Use your generalizations from Exercises 37 and 38 to write each of these expressions in factored form.

   a. $x^2 + 6x + 9$ **b.** $x^2 - 6x + 9$ **c.** $x^2 - 9$ **d.** $x^2 - 16$

40. Write each expression in factored form.

   a. $2x^2 + 5x + 3$ **b.** $4x^2 - 9$ **c.** $4x^2 + 12x + 9$

41. a. Find the areas of these circles.

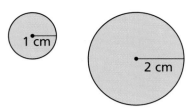

b. Copy and complete this table. Is the relationship between the area and the radius quadratic? Explain.

Radius (cm)	1	2	3	4	x
Area (cm²)	▪	▪	▪	▪	▪

c. Below are nets for two cylinders with heights of 2 meters. Find the surface areas of the cylinders.

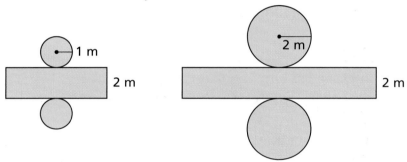

d. Copy and complete this table. Is the relationship between the surface area and the radius quadratic? Explain.

Radius (m)	1	2	3	4	x
Height (m)	2	2	2	2	2
Surface Area (m²)	▪	▪	▪	▪	▪

42. Multiple Choice The equation $h = 4 + 63t - 16t^2$ represents the height h of a baseball in feet t seconds after it is hit. After how many seconds will the ball hit the ground?

A. 2   **B.** 4   **C.** 5   **D.** 15

43. a. Complete the table to show surface areas of cylinders with equal radius and height. Use the nets shown.

Radius (ft)	1	2	3	4	x
Height (ft)	1	2	3	4	x
Surface Area (ft²)	■	■	■	■	■

b. Is the relationship between surface area and radius quadratic? Explain.

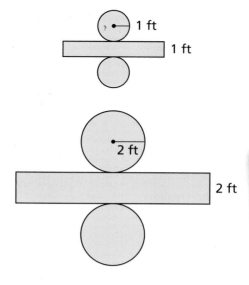

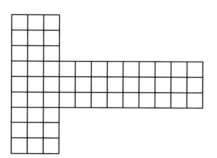

44. At the right is a net of a cube, divided into square units.

a. What is the edge length of the cube?

b. Find the surface area and volume of the cube.

c. Draw a net for a cube with a volume of 64 cubic units. What is the length of each edge of the cube? What is the surface area of the cube?

d. What formula relates the edge length of a cube to its volume? Is this relationship quadratic? Explain.

45. Silvio wants to gift wrap a cubic box that has edges measuring 16 inches. He has 10 square feet of wrapping paper. Is this enough to wrap the gift? Explain.

46. Multiple Choice Which table could represent a quadratic relationship?

F.

x	y
−3	−3
−2	−2
−1	−1
0	0
1	1
2	2
3	3

G.

x	y
−3	1
−2	2
−1	3
0	4
1	3
2	2
3	1

H.

x	y
1	0
2	2
3	6
4	12
5	20
6	30
7	42

J.

x	y
−1	10
0	7
1	4
2	1
3	4
4	7
5	10

47. Multiple Choice Suppose $y = x^2 - 4x$. If $y = 0$, what are all the possible values for x?

A. −4   **B.** 0   **C.** 4 or 0   **D.** −4 or 0

48. The cube buildings below are shown from the front right corner.

Building 1

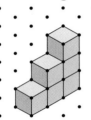

Building 2

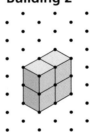

Building 3

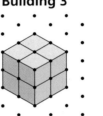

Building 4

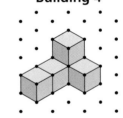

These drawings show the base outline, front view, and right view of Building 1. Draw these views for the other three buildings.

Base outline

Front view

Right view

49. Below are three views of a cube building. Draw a building that has all three views and has the greatest number of cubes possible. You may want to use isometric dot paper.

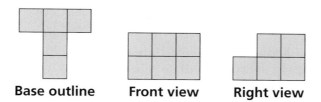

Base outline   **Front view**   **Right view**

50. Below are *base plans* for cube buildings. A base plan shows the shape of the building's base and the number of cubes in each stack.

Building 1

1	1	2
	3	1
	1	

Front

Building 2

1	1	2
1	3	
	1	

Front

Make a drawing of each building from the front right corner. You may want to use isometric dot paper.

Extensions

Use the following information for Exercises 51–53.

A soccer coach wants to take her 20-player team to the state capital for a tournament. A travel company is organizing the trip. The cost will be $125 per student. The coach thinks this is too expensive, so she decides to invite other students to go along. For each extra student, the cost of the trip will be reduced by $1 per student.

51. The travel company's expenses for the trip are $75 per student. The remaining money is profit. What will the company's profit be if the following numbers of students go on the trip?

    a. 20   b. 25   **c.** 60   **d.** 80

52. Let n represent the number of students who go on the trip. In parts (a)–(d), write an equation for the relationship described. It may help to make a table like the one shown here.

State Capital Trip

Number of Students	Price per Student	Travel Company's Income	Travel Company's Expenses	Travel Company's Profit
20	$125	20 × $125 = $2,500	20 × $75 = $1,500	$2,500 − $1,500 = $1,000
21	$124			

    a. the relationship between the *price per student* and n

    b. the relationship between the *travel company's income* and n

    c. the relationship between the *travel company's expenses* and n

    d. the relationship between the *travel company's profit* and n

53. Use a calculator to make a table and a graph of the equation for the travel company's profit. Study the pattern of change in the profit as the number of students increases from 25 to 75.

    a. What number of students gives the company the maximum profit?

b. What numbers of students guarantee the company will earn a profit?

c. What numbers of students will give the company a profit of at least $1,200?

54. A puzzle involves a strip of seven squares, three pennies, and three nickels. The starting setup is shown.

To solve the puzzle, you must switch the positions of the coins so the nickels are on the left and the pennies are on the right. You can move a coin to an empty square by sliding it or by jumping it over one coin. You can move pennies only to the right and nickels only to the left.

You can make variations of this puzzle by changing the numbers of coins and the length of the strip. Each puzzle should have the same number of each type of coin and one empty square.

a. Make drawings that show each move (slide or jump) required to solve puzzles with 1, 2, and 3 coins of each type. How many moves does it take to solve each puzzle?

b. A puzzle with n nickels and n pennies can be solved with $n^2 + 2n$ moves. Use this expression to calculate the number of moves required to solve puzzles with 1, 2, 3, 4, 5, 6, 7, 8, 9, and 10 of each type of coin.

c. Do your calculations for 1, 2, and 3 coins of each type from part (b) agree with the numbers you found in part (a)?

d. By calculating first and second differences in the data from part (b), verify that the relationship between the number of moves and the number of each type of coin is quadratic.

55. Complete parts (a) and (b) for each equation.

$y_1 = x + 1$ $y_2 = (x + 1)(x + 2)$

$y_3 = (x + 1)(x + 2)(x + 3)$ $y_4 = (x + 1)(x + 2)(x + 3)(x + 4)$

a. Describe the shape of the graph of the equation. Include any special features.

b. Describe the pattern of change between the variables.

56. The Terryton Tile Company makes floor tiles. One tile design uses grids of small, colored squares as in this 4 × 4 pattern.

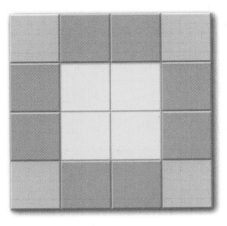

a. Suppose you apply the same design rule to a 5 × 5 grid. How many small squares will be blue? How many will be yellow? How many will be orange?

b. How many small squares of each color will there be if you apply the rule to a 10 × 10 grid?

c. How many small squares of each color will there be if you apply the rule to an $n \times n$ grid?

d. What kinds of relationships do the expressions in part (c) describe? Explain.

57. This prism is made from centimeter cubes. After the prism was built, its faces were painted.

How many centimeter cubes have

a. no painted faces?　　　　b. one painted face?

c. two painted faces?　　　　d. three painted faces?

e. How many centimeter cubes are there in all?

Mathematical Reflections 4

In this investigation, you looked at the relationship between height and time for several situations. You also looked for common features in the tables, graphs, and equations for quadratic relationships. These questions will help you summarize what you have learned.

Think about your answers to these questions. Discuss your ideas with other students and your teacher. Then, write a summary of your findings in your notebook.

1. Describe three real-world situations that can be modeled by quadratic functions. For each situation, give examples of questions that quadratic representations help to answer.

2. How can you recognize a quadratic function from
   a. a table?
   b. a graph?
   c. an equation?

3. Compare the patterns of change for linear, exponential, and quadratic functions.

Looking Back and Looking Ahead

Unit Review

In this unit, you studied quadratic relationships. You learned to recognize quadratic patterns in graphs and tables and to write equations for those patterns. You answered questions about quadratic relationships by solving equations and by finding maximum and minimum points on graphs.

Go Online
PHSchool.com

For: Vocabulary Review
  Puzzle
Web Code: apj-4051

Use Your Understanding: Algebraic Reasoning

Test your understanding and skill in working with quadratic relationships by solving these problems about a carnival.

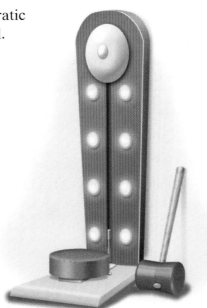

1. In the game pictured at the right, players hit the end of a lever with a mallet, propelling a weight upward. The player wins a prize if the weight hits the bell at the top.

   The height h of the weight in feet t seconds after the mallet strike is given by the equation $h = -16t^2 + bt$. The value of b depends on how hard the mallet hits the lever.

   a. Sketch the general shape of a graph of an equation of the form $h = -16t^2 + bt$.

   b. When Naomi plays, the weight rises 9 feet and falls back to the bottom in 1.5 seconds. Which table better matches this situation?

Table 1

Time (seconds)	0.0	0.25	0.5	0.75	1.0	1.25	1.5
Height (feet)	0	5	8	9	8	5	0

Table 2

Time (seconds)	0.0	0.25	0.5	0.75	1.0	1.25	1.5
Height (feet)	0	3	6	9	6	3	0

2. Wan's hit is hard enough to cause the weight to hit the bell. This situation is modeled by $h = -16t^2 + 32t$.

   a. How high did the weight go?

   b. How long did it take the weight to return to the starting position?

   c. When was the weight 12 feet above the starting position?

3. The carnival is adding pony rides for young children. They have 180 feet of fence to build a rectangular pony corral.

   a. Let x represent the length of the pony corral in feet. Write an expression for the width in terms of x.

   b. Write an equation that shows how the area A of the corral is related to its length x.

   c. What length and width will give an area of 2,000 square feet? Write and solve an equation whose solution is the required length.

   d. What length and width will give the maximum area? Explain how you could use a table or graph to find this maximum area.

Explain Your Reasoning

To solve Problems 1–3, you had to use your knowledge of quadratic functions and of tables, graphs, and equations for quadratic situations.

4. Suppose the relationship between x and y is a quadratic function. What patterns would you expect to see

   a. in a table of (x, y) pairs?

   b. in a graph of (x, y) pairs?

   c. in an equation relating x and y?

5. How are the equations, tables, and graphs for quadratic relationships different from those for

   a. linear relationships?

   b. exponential relationships?

6. How can you tell whether the graph of a quadratic equation of the form $y = ax^2 + bx + c$ will have a maximum point or a minimum point?

7. What strategies can you use to solve quadratic equations such as $3x^2 - 5x + 3 = 0$ and $x^2 + 4x = 7$ by using

   a. a table of a quadratic function?

   b. a graph of a quadratic function?

Look Ahead

Quadratic functions are models for several important relationships between variables. They are also among the simplest examples of nonlinear relationships. You will encounter quadratic functions in future *Connected Mathematics* units and in future mathematics and science courses.

C

constant term A number in an algebraic expression that is not multiplied by a variable. In the expanded form of a quadratic expression, $ax^2 + bx + c$, the constant term is the number c. The constant term in the expression $-16t^2 + 64t + 7$ is 7. The constant term in the expression $x^2 - 4$ is -4.

término constante Un número en una expresión algebraica que no está multiplicado por una variable. En la forma desarrollada de una expresión cuadrática, $ax^2 + bx + c$, el término constante es el número c. El término constante en la expresión $-16t^2 + 64t + 7$ es 7. El término constante en la expresión $x^2 - 4$ es -4.

D

Distributive Property For any three numbers a, b, and c, $a(b + c) = ab + bc$.

propiedad distributiva Para cualesquiera tres números a, b y c, $a(b + c) = ab + bc$.

E

expanded form The form of an expression composed of sums and differences of terms, rather than products of factors. The expressions $x^2 + 7x - 12$ and $x^2 + 2x$ are in expanded form.

forma desarrollada La forma de una expresión compuesta de sumas o diferencias de términos, en vez de productos de factores. Las expresiones $x^2 + 7x - 12$ y $x^2 + 2x$ están representadas en forma desarrollada.

F

factored form The form of an expression composed of products of factors, rather than sums or differences of terms. The expressions $x(x - 2)$ and $(x + 3)(x + 4)$ are in factored form.

forma de factores La forma de una expresión compuesta de productos de factores, en vez de sumas o diferencias de términos. Las expresiones $x(x - 2)$ y $(x + 3)(x + 4)$ están representadas en forma de factores.

function A relationship between two variables in which the value of one variable depends on the value of the other. The relationship between length and area for rectangles with a fixed perimeter is a function; the area of the rectangle depends on, or is a *function* of, the length. If the variable y is a function of the variable x, then there is exactly one y-value for every x-value.

función Una relación entre dos variables en la cual el valor de una variable depende del valor de la otra variable. La relación entre la longitud y el área para rectángulos con un perímetro fijo puede considerarse como una función, donde el área del rectángulo depende de la longitud, o es una función de ésta. Si la variable y es una función de la variable x, entonces hay exactamente un valor de y para cada valor de x.

L

like terms Terms with the same variable raised to the same power. In the expression $4x^2 + 3x - 2x^2 - 2x + 1$, $3x$ and $-2x$ are like terms, and $4x^2$ and $-2x^2$ are like terms.

términos semejantes Términos con la misma variable elevada a la misma potencia. En la expresión $4x^2 + 3x - 2x^2 - 2x + 1$, $3x$ y $-2x$ son términos semejantes y $4x^2$ y $-2x^2$ son términos semejantes

line of symmetry A line that divides a graph or drawing into two halves that are mirror images of each other.

eje de simetría Una línea que divide una gráfica o un dibujo en dos mitades que son imágenes especulares entre sí.

linear term A part of an algebraic expression in expanded form in which the variable is raised to the first power. In the expression $4x^2 + 3x - 2x + 1$, $3x$ and $-2x$ are linear terms.

término lineal Una parte de una expresión algebraica en la que la variable está elevada a la primera potencia, especialmente en la forma desarrollada de una expresión. En la expresión $4x^2 + 3x - 2x + 1$, $3x$ y $-2x$ son términos lineales.

M

maximum value The greatest y-value a function assumes. If y is the height of a thrown object, then the maximum value of the height is the greatest height the object reaches. If you throw a ball into the air, its height increases until it reaches the maximum height, and then its height decreases as it falls back to the ground. If y is the area of a rectangle with a fixed perimeter, then the maximum value of the area, or simply the maximum area, is the greatest area possible for a rectangle with that perimeter. In this unit, you found that the maximum area for a rectangle with a perimeter of 20 meters is 25 square meters.

valor máximo El mayor valor de y en una función. Si y es altura de un objeto lanzado, entonces el valor máximo de la altura, o simplemente la altura máxima, es la mayor altura que alcanza el objeto. Si lanzas una pelota al aire, su altura aumenta hasta que alcanza la altura máxima, y luego su altura disminuye a medida que vuelve a caer hacia la tierra. Si y es el área de un rectángulo con un perímetro fijo, entonces el valor máximo del área, o simplemente el área máxima, es la mayor área posible para un rectángulo con ese perímetro. En esta unidad, encontraste que el área máxima para un rectángulo con un perímetro de 20 metros es 25 metros cuadrados.

minimum value The least y-value a function assumes. If y is the cost of an item, then the minimum value of the cost, or simply the minimum cost, is the least cost possible for the item.

valor mínimo El valor más pequeño de y en una función. Si y es el costo de un artículo, entonces el valor mínimo del costo, o simplemente el costo mínimo, es el menor costo posible para ese artículo.

P

parabola The graph of a quadratic function. A parabola has a line of symmetry that passes through the maximum point if the graph opens downward or through the minimum point if the graph opens upward.

parábola La gráfica de una función cuadrática. Una parábola tiene un eje de simetría que pasa por el punto máximo si la gráfica se abre hacia abajo, o por el punto mínimo si la gráfica se abre hacia arriba.

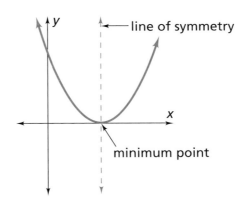

quadratic expression An expression that is equivalent to an expression of the form $ax^2 + bx + c$, where a, b, and c are numbers and $a \neq 0$. An expression in factored form is quadratic if it has exactly two linear factors, each with the variable raised to the first power. An expression in expanded form is quadratic if the highest power of the variable is 2. For example, $2x^2$, $3x^2 - 2x$, and $4x^2 + 2x - 7$ are all quadratic expressions. The expression $x(x - 2)$ is also a quadratic expression because $x(x - 2) = x^2 - 2x$. In this unit, you used quadratic expressions to represent the areas of rectangles for a fixed perimeter, the number of high fives between members of a team, and the path of a ball thrown into the air.

expresión cuadrática La expresión equivalente a una expresión de la forma $ax^2 + bx + c$, donde a, b, y c son números y $a \neq 0$. Una expresión en forma factorizada es cuadrática si tiene exactamente dos factores lineales, cada uno con la variable elevada a la primera potencia. Una expresión en forma desarrollada es cuadrática si la mayor potencia de la variable es 2. Por ejemplo, $2x^2$, $3x^2 - 2x$ y $4x^2 + 2x - 7$ son expresiones cuadráticas. La expresión $x(x - 2)$ también es una expresión cuadrática porque $x(x - 2) = x^2 - 2x$. En esta unidad, usaste expresiones cuadráticas para representar áreas de rectángulos para un perímetro fijo, el número de saludos entre los miembros de un equipo y el recorrido de una pelota lanzada al aire.

quadratic relationship A relationship between the independent and dependent variables such that, as the dependent values increase by a constant amount, the successive (first) differences between the dependent values change by a constant amount. For example, in $y = x^2$, as x increases by 1, the first differences for y increase by 3, 5, 7, 9, . . . and then the second differences increase by 2, 2, 2, ... The graphs of quadratic relationships have the shape of a U or upside down U with a line of symmetry through a maximum or minimum point on the graph that is perpendicular to the x-axis.

relación cuadrática Una relación entre las variables dependiente e independiente, de modo que, a medida aumentan los valores de la variable dependiente en una cantidad constante, las diferencias sucesivas (primera) entre los valores dependientes cambian en una cantidad constante. Por ejemplo, en $y = x^2$, a medida que x aumenta en 1, las primeras diferencias para y aumentan en 3, 5, 7, 9, . . . y luego las segundas diferencias aumentan en 2, 2, 2, ... Las gráficas de las relaciones cuadráticas tienen la forma de una U o una U invertida, con un eje de simetría que pasa por el punto máximo o mínimo de la gráfica perpendicular al eje de x.

quadratic term A part of an expression in expanded form in which the variable is raised to the second power. In the expression $4x^2 + 3x - 2x^2 - 2x + 1$, $4x^2$ and $-2x^2$ are quadratic terms.

término cuadrático Parte de una expresión en forma desarrollada, en la que la variable está elevada a la segunda potencia. En la expresión $4x^2 + 3x - 2x^2 - 2x + 1$, $4x^2$ y $-2x^2$ son términos cuadráticos.

term An expression that consists of either a number or a number multiplied by a variable raised to a power. In the expression $3x^2 - 2x + 10$, $3x^2$, $-2x$, and 10 are terms.

término Una expresión con números y/o variables multiplicados por una variable elevada a una potencia. En la expresión $3x^2 - 2x + 10$, $3x^2$, $-2x$, y 10 son términos.

triangular number A number that gives the total number of dots in a triangular pattern. The first four triangular numbers are 1, 3, 6, and 10, the numbers of dots in Figures 1 through 4 below.

número triangular Un número que da el número total de puntos en un patrón triangular. Los primeros cuatro números triangulares son 1, 3, 6 y 10, el número de puntos en las Figuras 1 a 4 de abajo.

Figure 1   Figure 2   Figure 3   Figure 4

English/Spanish Glossary

Academic Vocabulary

Academic vocabulary words are words that you see in textbooks and on tests. These are not math vocabulary terms, but knowing them will help you succeed in mathematics.

Las palabras de vocabulario académico son palabras que ves en los libros de texto y en las pruebas. Éstos no son términos de vocabulario de matemáticas, pero conocerlos te ayudará a tener éxito en matemáticas.

D

describe To explain or tell in detail. A written description can contain facts and other information needed to communicate your answer. A diagram or a graph may also be included.
related terms: express, explain, illustrate

Sample: Describe the graph of the equation $y = x^2 + 2x$.

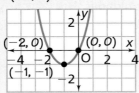

The graph of $y = x^2 + 2x$ is a parabola that opens up. The minimum is located at $(-1, -1)$. The y-intercept and one of the x-intercepts is at the origin. The other x-intercept is located at $(-2, 0)$.

describir Explicar o decir con detalle. Una descripción escrita puede contener hechos y otra información necesaria para comunicar tu respuesta. También se puede incluir un diagrama o una gráfica.
términos relacionados: expresar, explicar, ilustrar

Ejemplo: Describe la gráfica de la ecuación $y = x^2 + 2x$.

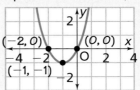

La gráfica de $y = x^2 + 2x$ es una parábola que se abre hacia arriba. El punto mínimo se localiza en $(-1, -1)$. El intercepto y y uno de los interceptos x están en el origen. El otro intercepto x-se localiza en $(-2, 0)$.

E

explain To give facts and details that make an idea easier to understand. Explaining can involve a written summary supported by a diagram, chart, or a table.
related terms: clarify, justify, tell

Sample: Darla factored the expression $x^2 + 15x + 56$. Explain what she did.

$$x^2 + 15x + 56 = x^2 + 7x + 8x + 56 \quad (1)$$
$$= x(x + 7) + 8(x + 7) \quad (2)$$
$$= (x + 8)(x + 7) \quad (3)$$

In Step 1, she rewrote 15x as the sum of 7x and 8x. In Step 2, she factored x from the first two terms and 8 from the last two terms. In Step 3, she factored $(x + 7)$ from both terms.

explicar Dar hechos y detalles que hacen que una idea sea más fácil de comprender. Explicar puede implicar un resumen escrito apoyado por un diagrama, una gráfica, o una tabla.
términos relacionados: aclarar, justificar, decir

Ejemplo: Darla factorizó la expresión $x^2 + 15x + 56$. Explica qué hizo.

$$x^2 + 15x + 56 = x^2 + 7x + 8x + 56 \quad (1)$$
$$= x(x + 7) + 8(x + 7) \quad (2)$$
$$= (x + 8)(x + 7) \quad (3)$$

En el Paso 1, volvió a escribir 15x como la suma de 7x y 8x. En el Paso 2, factorizó x de los primeros dos términos y 8 de los últimos dos términos. En el Paso 3, factorizó $(x + 7)$ de ambos términos.

P

predict To make an educated guess based on the analysis of real data.

related terms: estimate, guess, expect

Sample: Predict how many dots will be in Figure 8.

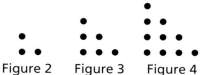

Figure 1   Figure 2   Figure 3   Figure 4

> Figure 1 has 1 dot. Figure 2 has 2 + 1 = 3 dots.
> Figure 3 has 3 + 2 + 1 = 6 dots. Figure 4 has
> 4 + 3 + 2 + 1 = 10 dots. If the pattern
> continues, figure 8 will have
> 8 + 7 + 6 + 5 + 4 + 3 + 2 + 1 = 36 dots.

predecir Hacer una conjetura informada basada en el análisis de datos reales.

términos relacionados: estimar, conjeturar, esperar

Ejemplo: Predice cuántos puntos habrá en la Figura 8.

Figura 1   Figura 2   Figura 3   Figura 4

> La Figura 1 tiene 1 punto. La Figura 2 tiene
> 2 + 1 = 3 puntos. La Figura 3 tiene
> 3 + 2 + 1 = 6 puntos. La Figura 4 tiene
> 4 + 3 + 2 + 1 = 10 puntos. Si el patrón
> continúa, la Figura 8 tendrá
> 8 + 7 + 6 + 5 + 4 + 3 + 2 + 1 = 36 puntos.

S

sketch To draw a rough outline of something. When a sketch is asked for, it means that a drawing needs to be included in your response.

related terms: draw, illustrate

Sample: The equation of the area of a rectangle is $A = w(20 - w)$, where w is the width of the rectangle in inches. Sketch a rectangle and a graph to represent the situation.

> Label one side of the rectangle w inches and the other side $20 - w$ inches.
>
> I sketched a graph of $A = w(20 - w)$ to show all of the possible areas of the rectangle.

hacer un bosquejo Dibujar un esbozo de algo. Cuando se pide un bosquejo, significa que necesitas incluir un dibujo en tu respuesta.

términos relacionados: dibujar, ilustrar

Ejemplo: La ecuación del área de un rectángulo es $A = w(20 - w)$, donde w es el ancho del rectángulo en pulgadas. Haz un bosquejo de un rectángulo y una gráfica para representar la situación.

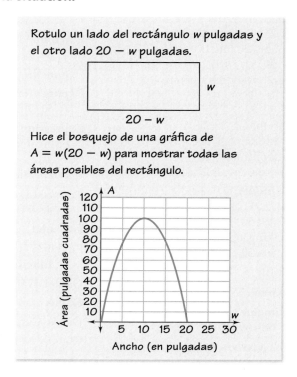

> Rotulo un lado del rectángulo w pulgadas y el otro lado $20 - w$ pulgadas.
>
> Hice el bosquejo de una gráfica de $A = w(20 - w)$ para mostrar todas las áreas posibles del rectángulo.

Academic Vocabulary

Index

Index

Index   **89**

Acknowledgments

Team Credits

The people who made up the **Connected Mathematics 2** team —representing editorial, editorial services, design services, and production services— are listed below. Bold type denotes core team members.

Leora Adler, Judith Buice, Kerry Cashman, Patrick Culleton, Sheila DeFazio, Richard Heater, **Barbara Hollingdale, Jayne Holman,** Karen Holtzman, **Etta Jacobs,** Christine Lee, Carolyn Lock, Catherine Maglio, **Dotti Marshall,** Rich McMahon, Eve Melnechuk, Kristin Mingrone, Terri Mitchell, **Marsha Novak,** Irene Rubin, Donna Russo, Robin Samper, Siri Schwartzman, **Nancy Smith,** Emily Soltanoff, **Mark Tricca,** Paula Vergith, Roberta Warshaw, Helen Young

Additional Credits

Diana Bonfilio, Mairead Reddin, Michael Torocsik, nSight, Inc.

Technical Illustration

WestWords, Inc.

Cover Design

tom white.images